German
for Singers

SCHIRMER
CENGAGE Learning™

German for Singers: A Textbook of Diction and Phonetics, Second Edition
William Odom and Benno Schollum

For product information and technology assistance, contact us at
Cengage Learning Customer & Sales Support, 1-800-354-9706

For permission to use material from this text or product, submit all requests online at **cengage.com/permissions**
Further permissions questions can be emailed to
permissionrequest@cengage.com

Library of Congress Control Number: 97020274

ISBN-13: 978-0-02-864601-5

ISBN-10: 0-02-864601-0

Schirmer
25 Thomson Place
Boston, MA 02210-1202
USA

Cengage Learning is a leading provider of customized learning solutions with office locations around the globe, including Singapore, the United Kingdom, Australia, Mexico, Brazil, and Japan. Locate your local office at: **international.cengage.com/region**

Cengage Learning products are represented in Canada by Nelson Education, Ltd.

For your course and learning solutions, visit **academic.cengage.com**

Purchase any of our products at your local college store or at our preferred online store **www.ichapters.com**

Printed in the United States of America
08 09 10 09 08

German
for Singers

A Textbook of Diction and Phonetics

SECOND EDITION

William Odom
University of Southern Mississippi

Benno Schollum
Wiener Hochschule für Musik und darstellende Kunst

SCHIRMER
CENGAGE Learning

Australia • Brazil • Japan • Korea • Mexico • Singapore • Spain • United Kingdom • United States

Contents

Preface to the Second Edition

Since *German for Singers* first appeared in 1981, it has enjoyed widespread acceptance by the singing profession. Reactions from users have led us to believe that the basic structure of the book enables the singer to acquire a mastery of German diction in a very efficient manner. For that reason, the main features of the original edition, as well as the organization of the materials, have been left largely unchanged.

Even though *German for Singers* has been an effective tool for thousands of singers, we nevertheless felt that the book needed some changes, clarifications, and improvements in order to produce a more thorough familiarity with the subtleties of German diction.

In this new edition, we have made several changes in IPA notation. For example, we have introduced the symbol for vowel length [ː], as in *beten* [ˈbeːtən]. Even though we point out that the length of a musical note will determine the length of the vowel, the fact is that, when using this book, singers will most often *speak* a word; and we felt that it was important to focus their attention on the quantitative difference between vowels as well as the qualitative difference. In making this change, as well as most other changes in IPA notation, we have generally brought our transcriptions more in line with those found in Siebs's *Deutsche Aussprache*.

In addition to changes in transcription, we have added some examples to the exercises and lists of exceptions and deleted others which were somewhat obscure. Mainly through the addition of footnotes, we have attempted both to recognize variations commonly accepted in the profession and to caution against others which are not. We have added the names of the poets for the song texts, and we have appended general guidelines followed by German-speaking singers for the pronunciation of Latin (Appendix C).

We would like to express our gratitude to John Maloy, chairman of the voice department at the Eastman School of Music, and Timothy Koch, choral director at the University of Southern Mississippi, for their support and for their invaluable suggestions.

Benno Schollum

The new co-author of *German for Singers*, Benno Schollum, brings with him a wealth of expertise and experience. Since 1982, Schollum has taught voice and diction at the Hochschule für Musik und darstellende Kunst in Vienna, and he regularly gives master classes at the Royal Academy of Music in London. In addition to his teaching, Schollum has maintained a very active performance schedule, singing in numerous European festivals and performing a variety of works under the baton of Yehudi Menuhin. His performance and subsequent recording of the Lieder cycle "Schein und Sein" (lyrics, Wilhelm Busch; music, Kurt Hueber) have been broadcast on radio and television, and his recent recordings of Schubert's "Winterreise" and Beethoven's Ninth Symphony (under Menuhin) have met with critical acclaim.

CD

This new edition includes a CD containing most of the materials in Chapters 1–9. The items included on the CD are indicated in the text by a CD icon (see left-hand margin). Frequently only certain portions of the items so marked appear on the CD.

The CD, which was recorded by Benno Schollum, offers the singer models of the most authentic German diction. The careful listener will note, as with any established singer, occasional deviations from the standard, but will find these variants mentioned in the text or footnotes. The listener will also note that Schollum uses the uvular *r* [R] throughout the recording. This practice is appropriate for natural spoken diction. In singing, of course, one should always use the trill [r].

Preface to the First Edition

This book has two main objectives: (1) to give the singer a systematic approach to pronouncing any German word; and (2) to provide the singer with a phonetic shorthand for making notations above trouble spots in a score.

A number of features have been introduced to assist the user in achieving these objectives.

International Phonetic Alphabet The *International Phonetic Alphabet* (IPA) is becoming an increasingly important tool in music diction. A number of foreign-language dictionaries and English dictionaries use IPA symbols to give pronunciations. Most diction manuals present the IPA for passive recognition only, as an aid in checking pronunciation in dictionaries. This text departs from this practice by providing exercises in transcribing into the IPA, as well as exercises in reading transcriptions. The intention is to provide singers with a tool which they can use throughout their careers to make notes on German scores or to help in languages with which they are unfamiliar. Singers always develop their own shorthand anyway, so it is well to guide them to a sure and universally accepted system early in their careers.

This book uses English examples to introduce the IPA. Since English-speaking singers already know the sounds, they can concentrate on learning the symbols. In addition, they should be able to retain the symbols more easily since they can associate them with familiar English words rather than foreign words.

The introduction to German pronunciation is greatly facilitated by knowing the IPA beforehand since most of the sounds of German are transcribed with symbols already mastered in the section on English phonetics. The symbols can thus serve as visual cues to the German sounds from the beginning.

Exceptions Included in every section on German pronunciation is a list of the exceptions to the rules, with their translations. Unfortunately, there are quite a few of these that occur regularly in vocal literature. The serious student is urged to memorize as many as possible.

Exercises The pronunciation exercises consist of words which contain the sound or sounds under discussion, including exceptions. If one spelling has more than one pronunciation, words in which the spelling is pronounced differently are mixed randomly in the exercises to assure that the student can recognize the conditions for the different pronunciations. The great majority of the examples have been culled directly from vocal literature, complete with endings and prefixes.

Excerpts Accompanying each section on German pronunciation are excerpts from vocal literature. In each case an attempt has been made to find excerpts which contain high concentrations of the letter or cluster under discussion and low concentrations of letters not yet treated.

Folk songs The folk songs, some of which are in fact simplified art songs, provide almost daily practice in singing German. Since they are musically very simple, they enable the student to focus on pronunciation. In most cases, songs have been chosen which have relatively high concentrations of the sounds discussed in the sections immediately preceding them.

Art songs The art songs in the body of the text and in Appendix B are intended for thorough preparation by the student. In general, they have not been chosen because they illustrate some phonetic point but rather because they are commonly performed by voice students. Since the songs are frequently heard and performed, the student will gain maximum long-range benefit from preparing them thoroughly, perhaps even memorizing them.

German for Singers is designed specifically for use in a three-hour university course. Because of its thorough treatment of phonetics, it can be used as the first in a sequence of diction courses in which a command of phonetics can then be assumed. If, however, training in phonetics is received elsewhere or if a two-hour course is offered, all of Part 1 and most of the transcription exercises in Part 2 can conveniently be eliminated.

    I must express my warmest thanks to Vivian Wood, without whose support, advice, and encouragement this book would have never been possible.

William Odom

CD Tracks

MODELS FOR GERMAN DICTION

CD Index	Start Time	Feature	CD Index	Start Time	Feature
1	00:00.0	Title	47	32:36.0	Ex.6.39
2	00:08.0	Ex.5.1	48	33:18.5	Excerpt 2
3	01:17.5	Ex.5.2	49	33:46.0	Ex.6.42
4	01:29.0	Ex.5.3	50	34:03.0	Exception 1
5	02:58.0	Ex.5.4	51	34:38.5	Ex.6.43
6	03:59.5	Ex.5.5	52	35:09.5	Exceptions
7	04:29.0	Excerpt	53	35:19.5	Ex.6.44
8	04:54.0	Ex.5.6	54	36:19.0	Excerpt 2
9	05:27.0	Ex.5.7	55	36:48.0	Ex.7.1
10	06:14.0	Ex.5.8	56	37:20.0	Ex.7.2
11	06:36.5	Excerpt	57	38:21.5	Inflectional Endings
12	07:19.0	"Am Brunnen"	58	38:42.5	words Ending in *er*
13	11:07.0	Ex.6.1	59	38:59.0	Ex.7.3
14	11:52.0	Ex.6.2	60	39:52.5	Ex.7.4
15	12:30.0	Ex.6.3	61	40:11.0	Ex.7.5
16	12:44.0	Ex.6.4	62	40:30.5	Ex.7.6
17	13:13.0	Ex.6.5	63	41:59.0	Ex.7.7
18	13:31.0	Section 1: Exceptions	64	42:38.5	Ex.7.8
19	13:44.5	Ex.6.8	65	43:10.5	Ex.7.9
20	14:32.5	Ex.6.9	66	43:26.5	Ex.7.10
21	15:07.5	Excerpt 2	67	43:54.5	Ex.7.11
22	15:25.5	"Du, du, liegst mir im Herzen"	68	44:11.0	Ex.7.12
23	17:05.0	6.12	69	45:21.0	Ex.7.14
24	18:07.5	Exceptions	70	46:27.0	Excerpt 2
25	18:38.0	Ex.6.14	71	46:58.0	Ex.8.1
26	20:18.0	Excerpt 2	72	47:33.5	Ex.8.2
27	20:42.0	Ex.6.20	73	48:40.0	Tape
28	21:07.0	Exceptions	74	49:20.0	Ex.8.4
29	21:35.0	Short *e* exceptions	75	50:01.0	Ex.8.5
30	21:52.5	Ex.6.22	76	51:10.0	Excerpt 3
31	22:36.0	Ex.6.23	77	51:40.0	Section 3 *g*
32	23:16.5	Ex.6.25	78	52:05.5	Ex.8.6
33	23:51.0	Ex.6.26	79	52:42.0	Ex.8.7
34	24:25.0	Ex.6.27	80	53:22.5	Ex.8.8
35	25:09.0	Excerpt 2	81	54:26.0	Excerpt 1
36	25:45.0	Ex.6.29	82	54:52.0	Exception 1
37	26:46.5	Exception 1	83	55:27.0	Ex.9.2
38	27:12.0	Ex.6.31	84	56:17.5	Ex.9.3
39	27:57.5	Ex.6.33	85	56:58.0	Excerpt 2
40	28:34.0	Ex.6.34	86	57:21.0	Exceptions
41	29:08.5	Ex.6.36	87	57:34.5	Ex.9.5
42	30:15.0	Excerpt 1	88	57:58.5	Ex.9.6
43	30:41.5	Ex.6.37	89	59:07.0	Excerpt 1
44	31:05.0	Exception 1	90	59:29.0	Section 3 *ie*
45	31:57.0	Ex.6.38	91	60:22.5	Section 3 *ien*
46	32:29.0	Exceptions	92	60:45.5	Excerpt 1
			93	61:01.5	Tapes

Alphabetical Index

Spelling		Pronunciation	Position	Examples	Page
a		[ɑː]	1. before *h*	ahnen ['ɑːnən] "to sense"	85
			2. doubled	Saal [zɑːl] "hall"	85
			3. before C	sagen ['zɑːgən] "to say"	85
			4. before CC in	Straße ['ʃtrɑːsə] "street"	86
			some words	zart [tsɑːrt] "gentle"	86
a		[a]	1. before CC	Mann [man] "man"	86
			2. before C in	an [an] "to, at"	86
			a few words	das [das] "that, the"	87
	ai	[ae]	all positions	Mai [mae] "May"	105
	au	[ao]	all positions	Haus [haos] "house"	105
	ay	[ae]	all positions	Bayer ['baeəʁ] "Bavarian"	105
ä*		[ɛː]	1. before *h*	Mähne ['mɛːnə] "mane"	90
			2. before C	spät [ʃpɛːt] "late"	90
			3. before CC in	zärtlich ['tsɛːrtlɪç] "gentle"	90
			a few words		
		[ɛ]	before CC	Händel ['hɛndəl]	90
	äu	[ɔø]	all positions	Häuser ['hɔøzəʁ] "houses"	106
b		[b]	1. before vowel, *l*	Eber ['eːbəʁ] "boar"	73
			or *r* in one element	geblickt [gə'blɪkt] "glimpsed"	73
			2. before *l, n,* or *r* in	ebne ['eːbnə] "level"	73
			derivatives or		
			inflected forms		
		[p]	1. final	Grab [grɑːp] "grave"	73
			2. preconsonantal	liebst [liːpst] "(you) love"	73
			3. final in element	Halbinsel ['halpˌɪnzəl] "peninsula"	73
				abreisen ['apˌraezən] "depart"	
	bb	[b]	in one element	Ebbe ['ɛbə] "ebb"	74
		[pb]	in two elements	abbauen ['apˌbaoən] "dismantle"	74
c		[ts]	before a front vowel	Cicero ['tsiːtseɾo]	136
		[k]	before a back vowel	Café [ka'feː] "cafe"	136
	ch	[χ]	after a back vowel	Bach [baχ] "brook"	28

C = Single consonant; CC = two or more consonants.

*The vowel *ä* is sometimes spelled *ae*; the pronunciation remains the same.

Spelling	Pronunciation	Position	Examples	Page
	[ç]	after a front vowel or a consonant	ich [ıç] "I"	137
			Mädchen ['mɛːtçən] "girl"	137
	[k]	in some words of Greek origin	Orchester [ɔrˈkɛstəʁ] "orchestra"	137
chs	[ks]	in one element	sechs [zɛks] "six"	141
	varied	in two elements	see Chapter 15	136
ck	[k]	all positions	nicken ['nɪkən] "nod"	131
d	[d]	1. before vowel or *r* in one element	Ader ['ɑːdəʁ] "artery"	76
			bedrohen [bəˈdroːən] "threaten"	
		2. before *l, n,* or *r* in derivatives or inflected forms	edler ['eːdləʁ] "noble"	76
	[t]	1. final	Freund [frɔønt] "friend"	76
		2. preconsonantal	widmen ['vɪtmən] "dedicate"	76
		3. final in element	fremdartig ['frɛmtˌɑːrtıç] "strange"	76
dd	[d]	in one element	Widder ['vɪdəʁ] "ram"	77
	[td]	in two elements	Raddampfer ['rɑːtˌdampfəʁ] "side-wheeler"	77
dt	[t]	in one element	Städte ['ʃtɛːtə] "cities"	76
	[tt]	in two elements	Handtuch ['hantˌtuːχ] "towel"	77
e	[eː]	1. before *h*	geht [geːt] "goes"	42
		2. doubled	Beet [beːt] "(flower)bed"	42
		3. before C	beten ['beːtən] "pray"	42
		4. before CC in some words	Erde ['eːrdə] "earth"	43
			stets [ʃteːts] "always"	
	[ɛ]	1. before CC	Bett [bɛt] "bed"	44
		2. before C in a few words	des [dɛs] "of the"	44
			weg [vɛk] "away"	
		3. in the prefixes *er-, her-, ver-, zer-*	erfahren [ɛʁˈfɑːrən] "experience"	44
	[ə]	1. final unstressed	Liebe ['liːbə] "love"	45
		2. medial unstressed	liebevoll ['liːbəfɔl] "loving"	45
		3. unstressed prefixes and endings	beginnen [bəˈgɪnən] "begin"	45
			meines ['maenəs] "of my"	45
ei	[ae]	in one element	mein [maen] "my"	105
eu	[ɔø]	in one element	Leute ['lɔøtə] "people"	105
ey	[ae]	in all positions	Meyer ['maeəʁ]	105
f	[f]	in all positions	fein [faen] "fine"	147
ff	[f]	in one element	treffen ['trɛfən] "meet"	147
	[ff]	in two elements	auffahren ['aofˌfɑːrən] "rise"	147
g	[g]	1. before vowel, *l,* or *r* in one element	Geld [gɛlt] "money"	80
			Glück [glʏk] "happiness"	80
		2. before *l, n,* or *r* in derivatives or inflected foms	eigner ['aegnəʁ] "own"	80

C = Single consonant; CC = two or more consonants.

Spelling	Pronunciation	Position	Examples	Page
	[k]	1. final	lag [lɑːk] "was lying"	80
		2. preconsonantal	klagt [klɑːkt] "laments"	80
		3. final in element	bergab [ˌbɛrkˈap] "downhill"	80
		4. in -ig before -lich	königlich [ˈkøːnɪklɪç] "royal"	80
	[ç]	in -ig when final or preconsonantal	heilig [ˈhaelɪç] "holy" heiligt [ˈhaelɪçt] "consecrates"	81
	[ʒ]	in some words of French origin	Genie [ʒeˈniː]	80
gg	[g]	in one element	Flagge [ˈflagə] "flag"	81
	[kg]	in two elements	weggehen [ˈvɛkˌgeːən] "go away"	81
gn	[gn]	in one element	Gnade [ˈgnɑːdə] "mercy"	81
h	[h]	initially in a word or element	Hand [hant] "hand" woher [voˈheːʁ] "whence"	121
	silent	elsewhere after a vowel	Floh [floː] "flea" gehen [ˈgeːən] "go"	121
i	[iː]	1. before h	ihn [iːn] "him"	35
		2. before C	mir [miːʁ] "me"	35
	[ɪ]	1. before CC	bist [bɪst] "(you) are"	36
		2. in the suffixes -in, -nis, -ig	Freundin [ˈfrɔøndɪn] "(girl) friend" Kenntnis [ˈkɛntnɪs] "knowledge" giftig [ˈgɪftɪç] "poisonous"	36
		3. in -ik if unstressed	Lyrik [ˈlyːrɪk] "lyrics"	36
		4. in some short words before C	mit [mɪt] "with" in [ɪn] "in"	36
ie	[iː]	all positions except final in some words	die [diː] "the" Melodie [meloˈdiː]	92
	[jə]	final in some words	Arie [ˈɑːrjə] "aria"	93
j	[j]	in most words	ja [jɑː] "yes" Major [maˈjoːr]	122
	[ʒ]	in some words of French origin	Journal [ʒʊrˈnɑːl]	122
k	[k]	in all positions	kaum [kɑom] "hardly"	130
kk	[k]	in one element	Akkord [aˈkɔrt] "chord"	131
kn	[kn]	in all positions	Knabe [ˈknɑːbə] "lad"	131
l	[l] (dental, "bright")	in all positions	hell [hɛl] "bright"	112
ll	[l]	in one element	fülle [ˈfʏlə] "fill"	112
	[ll]	in two elements	fühllos [ˈfyːlˌloːs] "unfeeling"	112
m	[m]	in all positions	mein [maen] "my"	149
mm	[m]	in one element	Flamme [ˈflamə] "flame"	149
	[mm]	in two elements	ummalen [ˈʊmˌmɑːlən] "repaint"	149
n	[n]	in all positions	nein [naen] "no"	149
ng	[ŋ]	in one element	Finger [ˈfɪŋəʁ]	150
	[ng]	in two elements	hingehen [ˈhɪnˌgeːən] "go there"	150
nk	[ŋk]	in one element	dunkel [ˈdʊŋkəl] "dark"	150

C = Single consonant; CC = two or more consonants.

Spelling		Pronunciation	Position	Examples	Page
		[nk]	in two elements	ankommen [ˈanˌkɔmən] "arrive"	150
	nn	[n]	in one element	Tanne [ˈtanə] "fir"	150
		[nn]	in two elements	annehmen [ˈanˌneːmən] "accept"	150
o		[oː]	1. before *h*	ohne [ˈoːnə] "without"	52
			2. doubled	Boot [boːt] "boat"	52
			3. before C	schon [ʃoːn] "already"	52
			4. before CC in some words	groß [groːs] "great" hoch [hoːχ] "high"	52
		[ɔ]	1. before CC	doch [dɔχ] "but"	53
			2. before C in a few words	ob [ɔp] "whether" von [fɔn] "of"	53
ö*		[øː]	1. before *h*	fröhlich [ˈfrøːlɪç] "merry"	48
			2. before C	schön [ʃøːn] "lovely"	48
			3. before CC in some words	größer [ˈgrøːsɐʁ] "greater" trösten [ˈtrøːstən] "console"	48
		[œ]	before CC	möchte [ˈmœçtə] "would like"	49
p		[p]	in all positions	Pein [paen] "pain"	126
	pf	[pf]	in all positions	Pfad [pfɑːt] "path"	126
	ph	[f]	in all positions	Phantasie [fantaˈziː]	127
	pp	[p]	in one element	Lippe [ˈlɪpə] "lip"	126
	ps	[ps]	in all positions	Psalm [psalm]	127
qu		[kv]	in all positions	Quarz [kvarts]	133
r		[ʁ]	1. final in some monosyllables	der [deːʁ] "the" mir [miːʁ] "me"	26
			2. in the suffix *-er*	bitter [ˈbɪtəʁ]	27
			3. in the prefixes *er-*, *her-*, *ver-*, *zer-*	vergessen [fɛʁˈgɛsən] "forget"	116
		[ɾ]	all other positions	fahren [ˈfɑːɾən] "drive" warten [ˈvaɾtən] "wait" Meer [meːɾ] "sea"	116
	rr	[ɾ]	in one element	sperren [ˈʃpɛɾən] "lock"	117
		[ʁɾ]	in two elements, as a rule	Vorrede [ˈfoːʁˌreːdə] "introduction"	117
s		[z]	1. before a vowel	singen [ˈzɪŋən] "sing"	95
			2. before *l*, *n*, or *r* in derivatives or inflected forms	unsre [ˈʊnzɾə] "our"	95
		[s]	1. final	Betrugs [bəˈtruːks] "of deceit"	95
			2. before a consonant	Dresden [ˈdreːsdən]	95
			3. final in element	Lesart [ˈleːsˌɑːrt] "version"	95
			4. before a vowel in some words	Erbse [ˈɛrpsə] "pea"	95
sch		[ʃ]	in one element	Schule [ˈʃuːlə] "school"	102

C = Single consonant; CC = two or more consonants.

* The vowel *ö* is sometimes spelled *oe*; the pronunciation remains the same.

Spelling	Pronunciation	Position	Examples	Page
	[sç]	in two elements	Röschen ['rø:sçən] "little rose"	102
sp	[ʃp]	initial in element	spielen ['ʃpi:lən] "play"	98
			Glockenspiel ['glɔkənˌʃpi:l]]	
	[sp]	1. medial or final in one element	Wespe ['vɛspə] "wasp"	98
		2. in two elements	Liebespaar ['li:bəsˌpɑːr] "couple"	98
			ausprägen ['ɑosˌprɛːgən] "stamp"	
ss	[s]	in one element	müssen ['mʏsən] "must"	97
	varied	in two elements	see Chapter 10	
ß	[s]	in all positions	muß [mʊs] "must"	96
			Muße ['mu:sə] "leisure"	
st	[ʃt]	initial in element	stellen ['ʃtɛlən] "place"	98
			verstellen [fɛrˈʃtɛlən] "disguise"	
	[st]	1. medial or final in one element	Laster ['lastəʁ] "vice"	100
			ist [ɪst] "is"	
		2. superlative -*st*	schnellste ['ʃnɛlstə] "fastest"	98
		3. in two elements	austragen ['ɑosˌtrɑːgən] "carry out"	100
t	[t]	in all positions	Tal [tɑːl] "valley"	129
th	[t]	in one element	Theater [teˈɑːtəʁ]	129
	[th]	in two elements	Rathaus ['rɑːtˌhɑos] "town hall"	129
ti	[tsɪ]	in the syllable -*tion*	Nation [naˈtsɪoːn]	129
tsch	[tʃ]	in one element	Deutsch [dɔøtʃ] "German"	129
tt	[t]	in one element	Fittich ['fɪtɪç] "wing"	129
	[tt]	in two elements	Bettag ['beːtˌtɑːk] "day of prayer"	129
tz	[ts]	in one element	setzen ['zɛtsən] "set"	123
	[tts]	in two elements	entzücken [ɛntˈtsʏkən] "delight"	123
u	[u:]	1. before *h*	Ruhe ['ru:ə] "rest"	54
		2. before C	Mut [mu:t] "courage"	54
		3. before CC in some words	Gruß [gru:s] "greeting"	56
			Buch [bu:χ] "book"	56
	[ʊ]	1. before CC	Kunst [kʊnst] "art"	57
		2. before C in some words	um [ʊm] "around"	57
			zum [tsʊm] "to the"	
ü*	[y:]	1. before *h*	fühle ['fy:lə] "feel"	39
		2. before C	für [fy:ʁ] "for"	40
		3. before CC in some words	Wüste ['vy:stə] "desert"	40
			grüßen ['gry:sən] "greet"	
	[ʏ]	before CC	fünf [fʏnf] "five"	40
v	[f]	in words of Germanic origin	viel [fiːl] "much"	145
	[v]	in most words of foreign origin	Vase ['vɑːzə]	146
w	[v]	in all positions	Wein [vaen] "wine"	143

C = Single consonant; CC = two or more consonants.

* The vowel *ü* is sometimes spelled *ue*; the pronunciation remains the same.

Spelling	Pronunciation	Position	Examples	Page
x	[ks]	in all positions	Hexe ['hɛksə] "witch"	133
y	[yː]	before C	Lyrik ['lyːrɪk] "lyrics"	37
	[ʏ]	before CC	idyllisch [i'dʏlɪʃ] "idyllic"	37
z	[ts]	in all positions	Zeit ['tsaet] "time"	123
			Kreuz [krɔøts] "cross"	
zz	[ts]	in words of Italian origin	Skizze ['skɪtsə] "sketch"	123

PART One **Phonetics**

1 Introduction to Phonetics

THE IPA

Consider the words *ski*, *key*, *quay*, *me*, *meat*, *meet*, *siege*, *seize*, *people*, and *amoeba*. They all contain the vowel sound traditionally represented in American dictionaries as ē.

Now consider the words *wage*, *wag*, *wad*, *wall*, *ago*, and *many*. Although the vowel *a* appears in each word, it represents a different sound in each; these sounds have been traditionally indicated as ā, ă, ä, ô, ə, and ĕ, respectively.

If we now include foreign languages in our discussion, it becomes clear that the sound ē has a number of yet different spellings and that the letter *a* has a number of yet different pronunciations. Although the number of sounds that human beings use in speaking is limited, it is apparent that the variety of spellings for these sounds can be bewildering. To facilitate the business of learning pronunciation, it would seem logical to have a system in which one symbol represents one sound. The International Phonetic Association, which was founded in 1886, had as one of its chief objectives to create just such a system. The result was the International Phonetic Alphabet, or IPA. Although not the only such alphabet, the IPA has become the most widely accepted one and is used in many of the standard references consulted by singers.

This textbook goes a step further than most diction manuals by giving the singer active practice in transcribing sounds into the IPA. Every singer needs a shorthand for jotting down pronunciations. As often as not, the singer will not copy a transcription directly from a reference book but will note down on a score a pronunciation which is troublesome or a correction given by a teacher or coach. In either event, it is convenient to have a ready command of the IPA in order to note down a pronunciation. Furthermore, if skill is achieved in writing the IPA, then it will be even easier for the singer to read transcriptions.

VARIATIONS IN SOUNDS

The exercises in the following chapters no doubt will generate lively discussions over which symbols to use in certain instances. Two factors must be taken into consideration in trying to resolve such questions.

First, one should consider the range of speech sounds as a continuum, much like the light spectrum. When we think of green, a variety of colors comes to mind. What we consider to be green is actually a somewhat arbitrarily chosen section of wavelengths which fades into yellow on one end and into blue on the other. Likewise, each IPA symbol represents not one sound but a family of closely related sounds. Thus the *t* sound is quite different in *top*, *stop*, *pot*, *rotten*, and *bottle* but will still be represented by [t] in the IPA.[1] Vowels also change their color depending on the nature of the consonants surrounding them. The *e* in *bed* does not have exactly the same sound as the *e* in *bet* or *bell*, but all may be represented by the IPA symbol [ɛ]. So, just as the word *green* can indicate a variety of shades, the symbols [t] or [ɛ] can indicate a range of sounds.

Second, the choice of a symbol for a certain sound is affected by individual pronunciation. Certainly, differences in accent will give rise to differences in pronunciation. But even within the same dialect group there are considerable differences in pronunciation. Individual differences can be well demonstrated with a spectrograph, or voiceprint, which is a printed recording of sound patterns. Although the voiceprint reflects aspects of speech other than pronunciation, it is theorized that a voiceprint, like a fingerprint, is not the same for any two people.

Confusion over the choice of symbols will be minimized if the students strive to represent not so much what they say but what they think the best singers would sing.

---

[1]The IPA has developed diacritic marks to reflect subtleties of difference, but they will not be used in this text.

2 Transcribing Sounds

THE SYMBOLS

Before we begin a discussion of transcription, a few notes on the conventions followed in transcribing are in order.

Sound versus Letter

A *sound* is always represented by an IPA symbol in square brackets: [t]; a *letter* is printed in italics: *t*.

Stress

The main, or primary, stress in a word is indicated by a vertical line above and to the left of the syllable, as in *intend* [ɪn'tɛnd]. The secondary stress heard in some words is indicated with a vertical line below and to the left of the syllable, as in *episode* ['ɛpɪˌsoʊd].

Length

In the IPA, *length* refers to the amount of *time* it takes to pronounce a sound, not to the quality of the sound. Thus the vowel in *mad* is actually longer than that in *mate*, although traditionally the sound of *a* in *mate* would be called "long *a*" and indicated as ā. In IPA transcription, length is indicated with a colon. The word *bead*, with a longer vowel sound, might appear in transcription as [biːd] and the word *beat*, with a shorter vowel, as [bit].

This concept of length is of little importance to the singer in English diction and will not be used in transcriptions. The situation in German is discussed in Chapter 6.

Symbols

One of the great advantages of the IPA is that it is based on the English alphabet. Many of the symbols for sounds are identical with the letters which represent the sounds. Thus the sound of the letter *t* is represented by the symbol [t]. The student should note that the following consonant symbols are used to denote the sounds most commonly associated with the letters of the same form: [b, d, f, g, h, k, l, m, n, p, r, s, t, v, w, z].

One Sound: One Symbol

When transcribing, do not be misled by spelling; always assign a symbol for each sound. Often, several letters are used to represent one sound, such as *ough* in *bought*, which is transcribed [bɔt]. Conversely, one letter may be used to represent two or more sounds, such as *x* in *fix*, which is transcribed [fɪks].

No punctuation, such as a capital or an apostrophe within a word, is reflected in IPA transcription. Thus *Pete's* is rendered as [pits].

VOWELS

Monophthongs

[i] and [ɪ]

The symbol [i] represents the sound of *i* in *ski*. It represents this sound regardless of how it is spelled. Thus we see that the words listed at the beginning of this section—*ski, key, quay, me, meat, meet, siege, seize, people, amoeba*—would be transcribed [ski, ki, ki, mi, mit, mit, siʒ, siz, pipəl, ə'mibə].

The symbol [ɪ] represents the sound of *i* in *skit*, which would be transcribed as [skɪt].

Exercise 2.1   Transcribe the following words:

1. pit, peat, Pete
2. bit, bits, bead, beads
3. nick, Nick, nix, nicks, Nick's
4. deep, dip, dips, dipped
5. be, been, bean, beans
6. fill, fills, filled, field
7. kick, quick, squeak, squeaked
8. sieve, seize, peace, piece, please

[ε] and [æ]

The symbol [ε] represents the vowel sound in *bed* [bεd]. The symbol [æ] represents the vowel sound in *cat* [kæt].

Exercise 2.2   Transcribe the following words:

1. bet, bat, fad, fads
2. bread, bred, breed, brad
3. guest, gassed, guessed, geese
4. ten, bend, banned
5. dint, dents, dance, dense
6. Nat's, gnats, nest, knack
7. incentive, indent, deeds, dens

Before the nasal sounds [m] and [n], [ɛ] becomes [ɪ] in some regional accents. Thus the pronunciation of *pen* and *pin* is the same: [pɪn]. If in doubt in some cases, consult a dictionary and always bear in mind that emulating the diction of the great singers is a sound approach.

Exercise 2.3   Read the following transcriptions aloud, then write down the words they represent. Some may have more than one spelling.

1. [spɪn, splin, tæks, spɛnd, ɛk'spænd]
2. [sɪnd, sɛnt, bægz, tækt]
3. [dɪ'kænt, kiz, friz, pær]
4. [rɪ'list, dɪ'siv, 'rɛspɪt, rɪ'sɪnd]
5. [tɛkst, pik, 'æˌspɛkt, 'klæsɪk, ɪm'prɛst]
6. [il, livz, 'dædɪ, 'frɛndlɪ, ækwɪ'ɛs]
7. [pæst, kwɪn'tɛt, prɪs'tin, prɪnts, 'pærɪs]

[ɑ] and [ɔ]   The symbol [ɑ] represents the sound of *a* in *father* ['fɑðər]. The symbol [ɔ] represents the vowel sound in *hall* [hɔl]. As with [ɪ] and [ɛ], there is a certain amount of overlap between [ɑ] and [ɔ], which varies from region to region and even from individual to individual. A norm should be sought with the help of dictionaries and good recordings.

Exercise 2.4   Transcribe the following words:

1. all, awl, fall, pause, paws
2. palm, calm, qualms, hot, pods
3. cot, caught, Don, dawn
4. clawed, clod, naught, not
5. far, for, park, pork
6. wrought, rot, rat, gnawed, nod

[ʊ] and [u]   The symbol [ʊ] represents the vowel sound in *book* [bʊk]. The symbol [u] represents the vowel sound in *boot* [but].

Exercise 2.5   Transcribe the following words:

1. nook, put, full, fool
2. moons, prove, route, foot
3. look, Luke, cooed, could, cod
4. lose, loss, lost, loose, loosed
5. crew, crude, crook, crock
6. baboon, monsoon, festoon
7. spool, pull, would, wood

[ʌ] and [ə]

The symbol [ʌ] represents the vowel sound in *but* [bʌt]. The symbol [ə], called the *schwa*, is the sound of *a* in *approve* [əˈpruv]. Although the articulation of the two sounds is somewhat similar, [ə] appears *only* in unstressed syllables.

Exercise 2.6   Transcribe the following words:

1. bun, blood, fussed, flux
2. abet, collect, condemn, vista
3. above, conundrum, alumnus, compulsive
4. walnut, muffled, enough, son, honey
5. buck, book, boot, putt, put, pool
6. symphony, sonata, funnel, accustomed

Exercise 2.7   Read the following transcriptions aloud, then write down the words they represent. Some may have more than one spelling.

1. [kəˈkafənɪ, ˈɑrɪə, ˈlʌvəbəl, ˈdæmzəl]
2. [kəˈdɛnzə, bəˈsun, ˈɑpərə, kwɑrˈtɛt]
3. [ˌrɛsɪtəˈtiv, ˌkʌlərəˈturə, kənˈklusɪv]
4. [ˈɔrgən, rʌf, kɔf, ˈhɪkəp, ˈɔfəl]
5. [ˈrɔkəs, du, luz, fʊlˈfɪl]
6. [brʊk, wʊlvz, lus, bru, ˈkrʊkɪd]
7. [lɔrd, lɑrd, hʊk, hɑk, hɔk]
8. [sɔt, sʊt, sɑt, sæt, sɛt]
9. [ɛgˈzɔst, brˈkɔz, fɑks, kɔt]

Diphthongs

The word *diphthong* comes from the Greek *di-*, "two," and *phthongos*, "sound." A diphthong is a vowel which begins with one sound and ends with another. Although only two of the English diphthongs are regularly spelled with two vowels, there are at least five diphthongs in English.

[ɔɪ] and [aʊ]

The diphthong [ɔɪ] is the vowel sound in boy [bɔɪ].

The diphthong [aʊ] is the vowel sound in *how* [haʊ]. Notice that we use the symbol [a] instead of the symbol [ɑ] for the first part of the diphthong. The pronunciation of the sounds [a] and [ɑ] will be discussed below.

Exercise 2.8   Transcribe the following words:

1. bough, boy, boil, bout
2. decoy, ploy, plough, exploit
3. abound, anoint, foist, Faust, clown
4. fowl, foul, foil, fool, full, folly, fun
5. crowd, proud, about, royal

[aɪ, eɪ, oʊ]

There are three other sounds which must be considered phonetically as diphthongs even though they are commonly assumed to be single sounds. These are [aɪ] as in *pile* [paɪl], [eɪ] as in *pale* [peɪl], and [oʊ] as in *pole* [poʊl]. Of course, these diphthongs have a variety of spellings, including some which apparently have a letter to represent the second element [ɪ] or [ʊ], such as *i* in *maid* [meɪd] or *w* in *low* [loʊ]. It is important to realize that there is no distinction in pronunciation between the vowel in *maid* and that in *made* and that both must be transcribed with the diphthong [eɪ].

Exercise 2.9   Transcribe the following words:

1. ways, weighs, wades, waits, straight
2. load, lode, lowed, dough, mouldy
3. write, right, slight, sleight, slate
4. height, weight, receive, weird
5. stole, stale, stile, style, steel
6. great, gray, mind, guide, aisle
7. sew, know, ago, sorrow, window

Exercise 2.10   Read the following transcriptions aloud, then write the words they represent. Some may have more than one spelling.

1. ['lɔɪəl, ə'baʊt, sleɪ, veɪn, roʊd]
2. [aɪl, laɪ, rɪ'freɪn, roʊm, rum, rʌm]
3. [taɪm, 'mɛdoʊ, loʊn, 'kwaɪət, oʊ, aʊ]
4. [baɪd, boʊd, beɪd, baʊd, bɔɪd, bid, bɪd, bæd, bɔd, bɛd, bud, bʌd]
5. ['soʊfə, aɪ, reɪn, kəm'pleɪn, soʊl]

English Diphthong versus German Monophthong

With the sounds [eɪ] and [oʊ], it is very important to be aware of the second elements [ɪ] and [ʊ]. In English, except in some unstressed syllables, these sounds always appear as diphthongs and never as the monophthongs [e] and [o]. In German, as well as in other major European languages, these sounds always appear as monophthongs. Contrast the following:

English	*German*
bait [beɪt]	Beet [bet]
boat [boʊt]	Boot [bot]

To pronounce the German words with the English vowels would result in a recognizable, and undesirable, accent. We will treat these sounds in greater detail in Chapter 6.

[ɑ] versus [a]

In the diphthongs [aɪ] and [aʊ], a new symbol, [a], is introduced. Though the sound it represents does not occur in isolation in standard American English, it can be isolated for the sake of contrast by pronouncing *lie* [laɪ] and eliminating the second element of the diphthong: [la]. The sound thus obtained is quite different from the sound in *la* [lɑ], [ɑ] being more of a back vowel and [a] being more of a front vowel. The sound [a] does exist in isolation in some accents, for example, in the New England pronunciation of *Harvard* [ˈhavəd] or in the Deep South pronunciation of *dry wine* [dra wan]. The two sounds also occur in isolation in German, although the differentiation is made more in speaking than in singing. This will be discussed further in Chapter 9.

CONSONANTS

The symbols for most consonant sounds are the same as the letters of the alphabet most commonly used to represent the sounds. Some letters, however, have more than one pronunciation, and certain groups of letters represent a single sound. In both cases, some new symbols are required to represent the sounds.

[j]

Although phoneticians are not in agreement on the classification of [j] and [w], calling them variously *semivowels* or *glides*, these sounds are treated in this text as consonants. The symbol [j] represents the sound of *y* in *yes* [jɛs] or the initial element of *u* in *use* [juz] or *fuse* [fjuz]. The sound has other spellings, which are illustrated in the following exercise.

Exercise 2.11   Transcribe the following words:

1. Yale, yak, yen, yield, yoke, yacht, yawl, yule

2. hue, hew, human, view, cute

3. beautiful, onion, music, accurate

4. due, news, neutral, suit, tune, consume

5. euphoria, feudal, futile, stew, stupid

[ŋ]

The symbol [ŋ] represents the sound of *ng* in *tang* [tæŋ] and *n* in *tank* [tæŋk]. Note that in the combination *ng*, *g* is sometimes pronounced, sometimes not, e.g., *finger* [ˈfɪŋgər], *singer* [ˈsɪŋər].

Exercise 2.12 Transcribe the following words:

1. swinging, fang, long, lung
2. sink, sank, sunk
3. hungry, angry, single, longer
4. ankle, inkling, donkey, monkey, uncle
5. concord, concubine, conclave, conquer
6. ingot, ingrate, pancake, spank

[ʃ] and [ʒ]

The symbol [ʃ] represents the sound of *sh* in *shot* [ʃɑt] or *ti* of the syllable *-tion*, as in *nation* ['neɪʃən]. The symbol [ʒ] represents the sound of *s* in *pleasure* ['plɛʒər] or *si* in *Asia* ['eɪʒə]. Both sounds have other spellings, which are illustrated in the following exercise.

Exercise 2.13 Transcribe the following words:

1. shad, shade, shed, shod, should, shied
2. passion, machine, fiction, fashion, fascist, sugar, issue, ocean, special
3. treasure, confusion, occasion, decision, prestige, garage
4. fusion, fission, fissure, concussion, glacier, glazier

Exercise 2.14 Read the following transcriptions aloud, then write the words they represent. Some may have more than one spelling.

1. ['eɪnʃənt, 'æʒur, du, dju, jʌŋ]
2. ['mɛʒər, 'mouʃən, ruz, ruʒ]
3. ['siʃɛl, ʃɪp'ʃeɪp, 'kɪŋdəm, 'ʃælou]
4. ['wɪŋɪd, 'jɛlou, jild, ʃip, jɪr]

[tʃ] and [dʒ]

The combined symbol [tʃ] represents the sound of *ch* in *chat* [tʃæt]; [dʒ] represents the sound of *j* in *joy* [dʒɔɪ]. Both sounds have other spellings.

Exercise 2.15 Transcribe the following words:

1. chants, chance, choke, choice, cheek
2. catch, ketch, cello
3. jam, judge, bridge, gem
4. batch, badge, just, gust, gist, jest
5. char, jar, ridge, rich, garage

[ɾ]

The symbol [ɾ] is used to represent the sound of *r* in the stereotypical English butler's "very [vɛɾɪ] good, sir." The sound, which is also represented by *rr*, is called a *one-tap trill*. Although this pronunciation is usually said to occur between vowels, very few Americans use it in that position, preferring instead [ɾ]. In actual practice, the American articulation of *t, tt* and *d, dd* between vowels is virtually indistinguishable from [ɾ]; thus *catty, caddy,* and *carry* might all be pronounced ['kæɾɪ], although convention dictates that we transcribe *t* or *tt* as [t] and *d* or *dd* as [d].

One position in which many Americans use the pronunciation [ɾ] for *r* is after *th*. If the words *three, throw* are pronounced quickly and forcefully, the one-tap trill can be clearly heard.

It is beyond the scope of this text to consider the significance of [ɾ] in singing English. This pronunciation of *r* is very important in German diction, however, and will be discussed in greater detail in Chapters 5 and 12.

[θ] and [ð]

The symbol [θ] represents the sound of *th* in *thin* [θɪn]. The symbol [ð] represents the sound of *th* in *then* [ðɛn].

Exercise 2.16   Transcribe the following words:

1. this, that, think, thin
2. thrift, three, brother, bother
3. wrath, rather, cloth, clothing
4. father, path, paths, pithy
5. throng, faith, Gothic, goatherd

Exercise 2.17   Read the following transcriptions aloud, then write the words they represent. Some may have more than one spelling:

1. ['weɪdʒər, wɪtʃ, 'ʃepərd, 'retʃɪd, rɛkt]
2. [heɪld, 'twaɪˌlaɪt, ɛk'spɪɾɪəns, 'prɑmptlɪ]
3. ['faðər, ə'nʌðər, 'tʃɑrmɪŋ, reɪndʒd, tʌŋz]
4. [juθ, dʒus, 'hɛlθ, 'θʌndrəs]
5. [stretʃ, 'freɪgrənt, 'stɛlθɪlɪ, bauz]
6. [θrɛd, θrʌst, 'blasəmz, 'mɪst, 'buzəm]
7. ['paɪəs, 'prɪðɪ, 'eɪndʒəl, rɪ'dʒɔɪs]
8. [fær'wɛl, sɔŋz, 'θauzənd, 'rʌʃɪŋ, dʒu'dɪʃəs]
9. [ðaɪn, tɪtʃ, hɑrt, eɪk, 'nʌθɪŋ, mjut]
10. [ɑrtʃt, dɛpθ, bouθ, tʃɔɪs, ðou]

3 Describing Sounds: Articulatory Phonetics

W hen learning the sounds of another language, it is desirable to describe the mechanical means by which sounds are formed. If a sound is articulated differently from its English analog, what do we do with our tongue, teeth, and lips to reflect this difference? The study of how sounds are produced is called articulatory phonetics.

It is logical to begin the study of articulatory phonetics by analyzing the sounds of one's own language, since the student can produce the sounds naturally and correctly and can then determine by feel how the speech apparatus is being employed to produce them. Having thus become consciously aware of the speech apparatus, the student can learn to control it and use it to produce unfamiliar sounds.

Appendix A on pages 154–56 contains charts which provide complete phonetic descriptions of each vowel and consonant. Refer to them for orientation, but do not memorize the descriptions. The main objective of this chapter is to make you aware of how you use your speech apparatus to produce sounds. Rote learning of phonetic descriptions will probably not help you toward this objective.

CONSONANTS

Although there is no universal agreement on just what a consonant is, we will adhere to a more or less traditional classification. A fairly complete description of the production of a consonant sound can be given with three items of information:

1. voicing

2. major articulators

3. manner of production

The sound [b], for example, is described as a *voiced bilabial stop*.

Voicing

When the vocal chords vibrate during the production of a sound, for example [z], the sound is said to be *voiced*. When they do not vibrate, as in the production of [s], the sound is said to be *voiceless*.

Exercise 3.1   Indicate whether the underlined letters in the following words represent voiced or voiceless consonants. Refer to the chart in Appendix A only to check yourself.

1. ton
2. den
3. bed
4. bet
5. pad
6. bad
7. his
8. this
9. thistle
10. bath
11. baths
12. pats
13. pads
14. boxes
15. vision
16. fission
17. edge
18. etch
19. rag
20. rack
21. win

Articulators

The second of the three terms used in the description of a consonant sound indicates the major articulators involved in its production. Below is a list of such terms. The role of the tongue is not normally reflected in the descriptive term. Figure 1 identifies the main apparatus for producing speech sounds.

Bilabial A bilabial consonant involves the use of both lips to stop or constrict the flow of breath, for example, [b] or [w].

Labiodental A labiodental consonant involves the upper teeth and lower lip in its production, for example, [f].

Dental In articulating a dental consonant, the tip of the tongue is brought into contact with the back of the upper teeth, as in [θ].

Alveolar An alveolar consonant involves the tip or blade of the tongue and the alveolar ridge in its production, as in [n] or [z].

Prepalatal A prepalatal consonant involves the tip or blade of the tongue and the area between the alveolar ridge and the hard palate, for example, [r] or [ʒ].

Figure 1.
Points of Articulation

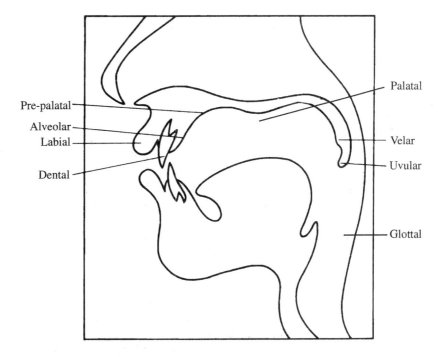

Palatal   A palatal consonant is produced with the blade of the tongue and the hard palate, as in [j].

Velar   A velar consonant is formed with the back of the tongue and the velum, or soft palate, for example, [k] or [ŋ]. Sometimes, especially in reference to German, the velar consonants are called *guttural* consonants.

Glottal   The glottis is the opening between the vocal chords. It is almost closed in the production of the glottal consonant [h].

Exercise 3.2   Describe the sounds represented by the underlined letters with one of the above terms.

1. ba̱ll
2. c̱at
3. vi̱sion
4. ṉut
5. ti̱p
6. w̱olf
7. thi̱nk
8. do̱g
9. ho̱t
10. y̱es
11. fi̱ssion
12. la̱ser
13. f̱ind
14. ṯhin
15. ṯon
16. ba̱d
17. v̱olt
18. ṉama
19. ṟip
20. pa̱ths

Manner of Production

In the preceding section we discussed the apparatus involved in producing speech sounds. We now need to describe how the apparatus is used to produce the sounds. Although [t] and [s] may both be described as alveolar and voiceless, it is clear that we are using the same apparatus to do two quite different things.

Below is a list of terms which describe the manner in which consonant sounds are produced.[1]

Stop In the production of a stop, all air flow is stopped momentarily by a set of articulators and then released, as in [b] or [k]. Stops are also called *plosives*.

Fricative A fricative is the type of sound produced by directing the air flow past a set of articulators without stopping it as in [s], [v], or [θ]. Fricatives are sometimes also called *spirants*. The *s*-like fricatives [s], [z], [ʃ], and [ʒ] are occasionally referred to as *sibilants*.

Affricate An affricate is a consonant sound consisting of two sounds spoken rapidly together, for example, [tʃ] and [dʒ]. An affricate consists of a stop which is released as a fricative.

Nasal In the production of a nasal, the flow of air is directed through the nasal passages, as in [m] or [ŋ].

Lateral In the production of a lateral, the air flow is directed over the sides of the tongue, as in [l].

Glide The English glides are [w] and [j]. It was pointed out above that the definition of a consonant is problematic. The glides, which are sometimes called semivowels, are part of the problem. When pronouncing the word *we,* we notice that it consists of a very brief [u] followed by [i]. The sounds [w] and [j] fail certain tests for vowels, however, and will be classified in this text as consonants.

Retroflex A retroflex sound is produced with the tip of the tongue curled back, as in English [r].

Trill A trill is the rapid contact between the tip of the tongue and the alveolar ridge or between the uvula and the back of the tongue. In singing, only the former type is considered. English has only the one-tap trill [ɾ]. In other languages, notably Italian, this [ɾ] may be trilled a number of times in rapid succession, producing the trill [r].

---

[1]Additional terminology:

   Aspiration Aspiration generally refers to the puff of air that follows a consonant, e.g., [p, t, k] in English or German. In the Romance languages, this aspiration is usually absent.

   Liquid The consonants *l* and *r* are sometimes referred to as liquids, regardless of articulation.

Exercise 3.3   Using the above terms, give the manner of production for the sounds represented by the underlined letters.

1. pot
2. school
3. vat
4. that
5. man
6. sank
7. fin
8. fission
9. kitchen
10. chair
11. vision
12. blizzard
13. rash
14. thrash
15. dun
16. dug
17. bell
18. yet
19. wolf
20. rigid

Exercise 3.4   Write the IPA symbol for the sounds described as follows:

1. voiced bilabial stop
2. voiced dental fricative
3. voiceless velar stop
4. voiced alveolar nasal
5. voiced palatal glide
6. voiceless alveolar fricative

Exercise 3.5   Give complete, three-part descriptions of the sounds represented by the underlined letters.

1. spot
2. pithy
3. three
4. think
5. dim
6. wet
7. visible
8. fission
9. fusion
10. bell
11. reef
12. feel

VOWELS

Defining a vowel can be problematic because one has some latitude in deciding what criteria to use. This text will sidestep the question and accept the traditional division of vowels and consonants with a caution to the student that in some ways and in some instances this division is almost arbitrary.

Vowel Description

In the pronunciation of vowels, the tongue is usually in an arched position with the tip pointing down. Although the entire tongue changes position in pronouncing different vowels, it is convenient to use the position of the peak,

Figure 2.
Tongue Position for Vowels

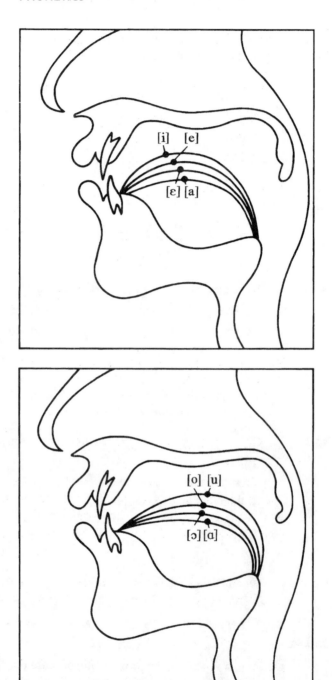

or highest point, of the tongue arch in describing vowel sounds. Figure 2 shows the shape of the arch for certain vowels, with the dot indicating the peak for each.

If we now consider the peaks alone, we see that they can be arranged schematically as in Figure 3. From Figures 2 and 3 it can be seen that [i, e,

Figure 3.
Schematic Position of Peak of
Tongue Arch

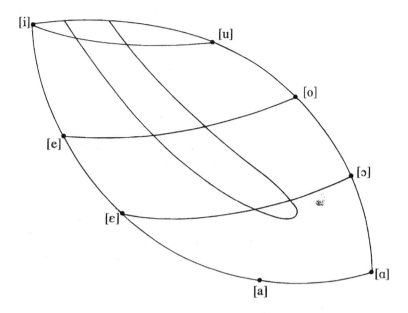

ɛ, a]² are arranged roughly along a line sloping upward toward the front of the mouth and that [u, o, ɔ, ɑ] are arranged roughly along a line sloping less sharply upward toward the back of the mouth, the whole configuration vaguely suggesting the form of a trapezoid that has [i, a, ɑ, u], called the cardinal vowels, as its corners (see Figure 4). For the sake of reference, it is convenient to arrange all the vowels within or along the boundaries of a trapezoid, as in Appendix A, Chart 3.

From Appendix A, Chart 3, we see that we can pinpoint the position of the peak of the arched tongue in somewhat the same manner as we locate a point on a grid, by giving its horizontal position (front, central, back) and its vertical position (high, mid, low). Thus we see that [i] may be described as a *high front vowel.*

Exercise 3.6   Describe the vowel sounds represented by the underlined letters according to the above terminology. Use the chart in Appendix A only to check yourself.

1. k<u>ee</u>d   6. c<u>ou</u>ld
2. k<u>i</u>d   7. c<u>oo</u>ed
3. c<u>a</u>d   8. c<u>u</u>d
4. c<u>o</u>d   9. c<u>a</u>denza
5. c<u>aw</u>ed

²You will recall that the sounds [e, a, o] do not commonly occur in isolation but only in the diphthongs [eɪ, aɪ, aʊ, oʊ] in standard American English. They do, however, occur in isolation in German.

Figure 4.
Cardinal Vowels

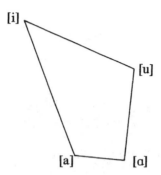

Quality

Another factor must be considered in the description of a vowel, in addition to tongue position. This is known as *tension* or *closeness*. The difference between [i] and [ɪ], for example, lies not only in the fact that for [ɪ] the tongue is drawn farther down and back. In the production of [i] the muscles of the lips and tongue are under tension. With [ɪ], the lips and tongue are more relaxed.

The vowel [i] is said to be *tense*, or *closed*; the vowel [ɪ] is *lax*, or *open*. (Although *tense* and *lax* are more descriptive terms, this text will use *closed* and *open* since these terms are traditionally used in describing German vowels.) The contrast can be felt physically by placing the finger lightly on the chin or by placing the thumb on the tongue muscle under the lower jaw and pronouncing the two sounds in succession. The following are contrasting pairs of vowels:

Front		**Back**	
closed	*open*	*closed*	*open*
[i]	[ɪ]	[u]	[ʊ]
[e]	[ɛ]	[o]	[ɔ]

It is important to understand the distinction between closed and open vowels because it plays an important role in German diction.

Exercise 3.7   Identify the vowels in the following words as closed or open:

1. wooed, would, full, fool, push
2. hole, hall, code, cawed, home
3. bet, bait, wade, wed, pen
4. seat, sit, list, leased, seize
5. frost, pose, pill, do, vault

Two The Sounds of German

CHAPTER

4 **Introduction**

n many respects, German is an easy language to pronounce for speakers of English. It, like Italian, is commonly said to be a "phonetic" language; that is, for each spelling there are normally no more than one or two pronunciations, and, conversely, for each pronunciation there are usually no more than one or two spellings. Contrast this situation with English, which has, as we pointed out in Chapter 1, at least ten spellings for the sound [i] and at least six pronunciations for the letter *a*.

Even when there are two pronunciations for a letter in German, it is fairly easy for the singer to recognize from the position of the letter in the word and from the letters following it which pronunciation is to be chosen. In some instances it will be necessary to recognize certain prefixes or verb endings in order to choose the right pronunciation.

ORGANIZATION

Since German is a fairly phonetic language and since one of the singer's main objectives in a study of German diction is to learn to pronounce German words printed in a score, the arrangement in this book is based on *spellings*—written symbols—rather than on sounds. Thus, even though *c* and *z* or *ie* and *i* may sometimes be pronounced alike, they are treated in different sections.

This text departs from the traditional approach of treating vowels and consonants completely separately. It instead treats the letters and their pronunciations in the order of decreasing difficulty. The difficult consonants *ch* and *r* are treated first, then the difficult closed and open vowels. The treatment of vowels is followed by a discussion of word structure, which will facilitate the differentiation of sounds; then concluding chapters on vowels and consonants are presented.

STANDARD REFERENCE

Students of German diction are fortunate in having at their disposal a definitive reference work designed for use by professional German actors, singers, and announcers. It is *Deutsche Aussprache* by Theodor Siebs, published by Walter de Gruyter & Co. (ISBN 3-11-000325-2). Most college or university libraries will have a copy, and the serious student should acquire a personal copy from the outset. Siebs provides pronunciations in IPA transcription of most German words and foreign words common to German, as well as transcriptions of a large number of proper names. In general, *German for Singers* will follow Siebs, but in a few instances it departs from the transcriptions in Siebs for the sake of greater clarity.

GENERAL RULES

Before beginning a detailed study of German sounds, the singer should become familiar with a few general rules regarding pronunciation and orthography.

Pronunciation like English In general, the singer may assume that the following consonants are pronounced as in English: *b, ck, d, f, g, h, k, m, n, p, t, x.* Exceptions will be discussed under the individual consonants.

Double consonants In spoken German double consonants are generally pronounced the same as single consonants; in singing they are somewhat more protracted.

Unvoicing The voiced consonants *b, d, g, s* are usually unvoiced in final position or before a consonant, for instance *d* in *Bad* [baːt], *g* in *legt* [leːkt]. As one might expect, there is a slight difference in articulation between a *t* and an unvoiced *d*, but the difference is subtle and will not be discussed in this book.

Word structure The division of words into their component parts can affect vowel quality and unvoicing as well as the pronunciation of double consonants and consonant clusters. Word structure is discussed further in Chapter 7.

Capitalization The student will note that many words in the following examples and exercises are capitalized. In German, all nouns are capitalized, including common nouns such as *Baum* "tree," *Geist* "spirit," etc.

Umlaut The umlaut letters *ä, ö, ü* are also spelled *ae, oe, ue* in some scores. There is no difference in pronunciation.

[ə] – think supported (↑ɛ̂↓)

[ɻ] –

CHAPTER

5 **The Sounds of *r, ch***

I t is best to begin the treatment of German pronunciation with the difficult consonants *r* and *ch*. The exercises in subsequent chapters can then include these consonants and provide ongoing practice in their articulation. A review and conclusion of the sounds discussed in this chapter will be found in Chapters 12 and 15.

SECTION 1:   *r, rr* (Part 1)

Speaking versus Singing

In speaking, the pronunciation of *r* before a vowel is uvular in most German-speaking areas; that is, it involves contact between the far back part of the tongue and the uvula, producing a gargling sound. The uvular pronunciation (IPA [R]) is used in singing popular songs but should be avoided in art songs and opera. The one-tap trill, or flipped *r* [ɾ], should be used instead.

In other positions, the pronunciation of *r* in speaking is more vowel-like in quality. The conditions for the use of this latter pronunciation in singing are not as clearly defined as those for most German sounds, and the singer is left a certain amount of latitude in its use.

Prevocalic: [ɾ]

The letter *r* should generally be pronounced as a one-tap trill when it stands before a vowel (and in spoken German it is pronounced this way in some parts of Austria, Switzerland, and southern Germany): *raten* ['rɑːtən] "guess," *beraten* [bə'rɑːtən] "advise." (Apparent exceptions to this rule are covered in Chapters 7 and 12.)

In noncompound words, the articulation of *rr* is the same as that for *r*, but it is more intense and lengthened slightly: *Karre* ['karə] "cart" (see also Chapter 12).

The singer should take care to tap the tongue only once against the lower part of the alveolar ridge. Some singers occasionally roll this trill as for the

Italian or Spanish *rr.* In German diction, this articulation should be avoided at first. Any decision to experiment with it should be based on many hours of critical listening to established singers.

Exercise 5.1

Pronounce the following words, following the rules for the pronunciation of *r* and *rr:*

1. Rand
   rasch
   Rest
   retten
   ringen
   Reigen
   rauschen
   Reue

2. Karre
   irren
   fahren
   ihren
   sperren
   führen
   lauere
   eure

3. aufragen
   Abreise
   Hauptrolle
   bereue
   gerissen

4. fragen
   Kragen
   tragen
   dreist
   graben
   Preis
   Schrift
   bringen

Exercise 5.2

Read the following excerpt:

Laß irre Hunde heulen, vor ihres Herren Haus...

Winterreise
Müller/Schubert

Final Position in Some Words and Syllables: [ʁ][1]

The other pronunciation of *r* is in effect a vowel sound which can be viewed as a variant of schwa ([ə]). The tongue is drawn back a little farther than for schwa, producing a back vowel which is very close to the sound of *o* in the British pronunciation of the word *hot* [hɒt]. We will use the symbol [ʁ] to designate this vocalic articulation of *r.*[2] In the articulation of schwa, the tip of

---

[1]Most references do not differentiate between the two types of *r,* using the symbol [r] for both. However, the singer is urged to adopt both [ɾ] and [ʁ] in making phonetic notations in order to reflect the difference in articulation.

[2]Siebs uses [ʁ] to indicate a *uvular* articulation. In general, however, the symbol appears in the Siebs entries in the same positions described here: the singer need only remember to use the more vocalic articulation.

the tongue is normally pointed down; in the articulation of [ʁ], the tongue should be pointed at, but not touching, the alveolar ridge. In this manner, the relationship of [ʁ] to the one-tap trill [ɾ] is maintained, and the articulations may be easily interchanged as style requires.

There are no hard and fast rules regarding the use of [ʁ]. Indeed, some singers almost never use it. However, most singers now make judicious use of [ʁ], especially in the nineteenth-century art song. As a rule of thumb, let us say that *r* will be pronounced [ʁ] in the following cases:

1. the article *der* [deːʁ] "the"
2. the pronouns
    mir [miːʁ] "me"
    dir [diːʁ] "you"
    er [eːʁ] "he"
    ihr [iːʁ] "her" or "you"
    wir [viːʁ] "we"
    wer [veːʁ] "who"
3. the prepositions
    für [fyːʁ] "for"
    vor [foːʁ] "before"
4. the prefixes
    er- [ɛʁ]
    ver- [fɛʁ]
    zer- [tsɛʁ]
5. the suffix *-er* [əʁ]

Suffix *-er*: [əʁ]

The suffix *-er* is pronounced [əʁ], as in *bitter* ['bɪtəʁ] "bitter." This suffix may also occur before other suffixes or endings beginning with consonants, as in *bitterster* ['bɪtəʁstəʁ] "bitterest" or in verb forms such as *flattern* ['flatəʁn] "flutter," *wandern* ['vandəʁn] "wander."

The suffix *-er* should not be confused with the prefix *er-*, which is always pronounced [ɛʁ], as in *erfahren* [ɛʁˈfɑːrən] "experience."

Other Positions: [ɾ]

In positions other than those described above, *r* should be pronounced as the one-tap trill [ɾ] (see Chapter 12).

Exercise 5.3

Pronounce the following words, using [ʁ] for *r* in the recommended words and syllables:

1. der, wer, mir, ihr, wir
2. erfahren, erkennen, verkleiden, derselbe, versagen
3. Lieder, leider, Vater, Meistersinger, Wagner, Wiener, immer, besser, Musiker, Orchester, Walter, Ritter, Retter, Wunder, Kindergarten
4. wandern, wanderst, wandert, wanderten, verbessert, mildert, flatterte, bit-terlich

Exercise 5.4

Final *e* is pronounced [ə] in German (see Chapter 6, "Section 3"). Practice contrasting [ə] and [əʁ] in the following pairs:

1. Messe	Messer
2. spiele	Spieler
3. gute	guter
4. Liede	Lieder
5. Leide	leider
6. Liebe	lieber
7. Treue	treuer
8. meiste	Meister
9. blaue	blauer

Exercise 5.5

Transcribe the following words into the IPA, using [ɾ] or [ʁ]:

1. Lieder, Bier, Rest, Retter, Kraft
2. Ritter, wandern, irren, Schubert, Bruckner

Excerpt

Read the following passage aloud, paying special attention to the pronunciation of *r*:

So wie dort in blauer Tiefe,
Hell und herrlich, jener Stern,
Also er an meinem Himmel,
Hell und herrlich, hehr und fern.

Frauenliebe und Leben
Chamisso/Schumann

SECTION 2: *ch* (Part 1)

There are two distinctly different pronunciations of *ch,* which should never be confused with each other.

[χ]

The sound [χ] is a voiceless velar fricative, a heavily aspirated [h], as in *Bach* [baχ]. This pronunciation of *ch* occurs after the back vowels *a, o, u, au.* It is commonly referred to in German as the *ach-Laut* ("*ach*-sound").

Exercise 5.6

Pronounce the following words, using [χ] for *ch*:

1. ach, machen, Pracht, Nacht, gemacht
2. Loch, noch, doch
3. auch, Rauch, Raucher
4. Buch, Kuchen, suchen

[ç]

The sound [ç] is a voiceless palatal fricative. The tongue is in the same position as for [j], but air is passed over it, producing a hissing sound. The sound is very much like the initial sound in the English words *hue, huge,* and *human,* as pronounced in standard American English. The pronunciation [ç] is used in German after consonants and after the front vowels, that is, after all vowels other than *a, o, u, au.* It is commonly referred to in German as the *ich-Laut* ("*ich*-sound").

Other pronunciations for *ch* will be treated in the conclusion of the discussion of *ch* in Chapter 15.

Exercise 5.7

Pronounce the following words, using [ç] for *ch*:

1. rächen, Becher, brechen, riechen, ich, mich
2. nicht, Angesicht, schleichen, Eiche, euch, feucht
3. mancher, Milch, welcher, Kelch
4. schnarchen, Lerche, Liebchen, Männchen

Exercise 5.8

Transcribe the following words into the IPA (*ä* = [ɛ]):

1. ich, ach, Becher, nicht, Milch
2. Nacht, Nächte, Bach, Bäche

Excerpt

Read the following passage aloud, paying special attention to the pronunciation of *ch*. Note: *ä* = [ɛ]; *v* = [f]; and *eu* = [ɔɪ]—approximately (see Chapter 11):

Kommt das grämliche Gesicht,
Kommt die Alte da mit Keuchen,
Lieb' und Lust mir zu verscheuchen,
Eh' die Jugend mir gebricht?
Ach! die Mutter ist's die aufwacht,
Und den Mund zu schelten aufmacht,
Nein, die Karten lügen nicht!
Die Kartenlegerin
Chamisso/Schumann

Tape

Practice speaking the text of the following song until you can read it through without errors. Then read the text onto a tape without stopping the recorder; if you make a mistake, start over. Note: *st* = [ʃt]; *z* = [ts].

Song

Sing the following song. Pay careful attention to the contrasts [r]:[ʁ] and [χ]:[ç].

Am Brunnen vor dem Tore

Am Brun - nen vor dem To - re   da steht ein Lin - den -
Ich mußt' auch heu - te wan - dern   vor - bei in tie - fer
Die kal - ten Win - de blie - sen   mir grad' ins An - ge -

baum, ich träumt' in sein - em Schat - ten   so man - chen sü - ßen
Nacht, da hab' ich noch im Dun - keln   die Au - gen zu - ge -
sicht; der Hut flog mir vom Kop - fe,   ich wen - de - te___ mich

Traum; ich schnitt in sei - ne Rin - de   so man - ches lie - be
macht; und sei - ne Zwei - ge rausch - ten   als rie - fen sie mir
nicht. Nun bin ich man - che Stun - de   ent - fernt von je - nem

Wort,   es   zog   in   Freud' und   Lei - de   zu
zu: Komm her   zu mir Ge - sel - le,   hier
Ort,   und   im - mer hör' ich's rau - schen: Du

ihm ____ mich im - mer   fort,   zu   ihm ____ mich im - mer fort.
find'st ____ du dei - ne   Ruh,   hier find'st ____ du dei - ne Ruh.
fän - dest Ru - he   dort,   du   fän - dest Ru - he dort.

6 Monophthongs—Part One: Long and Closed or Short and Open

C ertain monophthongs are generally *either* long and closed *or* short and open. This group consists of *i, ü,* (and *y*), *e, ö, o,* and *u*.

The vowels *a, ä,* and as a general rule *ie,* are also monophthongs; but since they do not reflect the same patterns of length and quality as the vowels of this chapter, they are not discussed here (see Chapter 9).

DIPHTHONGIZATION

In Chapter 2, it was pointed out that the English vowels generally assumed to be monophthongs frequently have a diphthongal element. This is almost universally true of the vowels commonly referred to as "long *a*" [eɪ] and "long *o*" [oʊ]. It is also true of other vowels to a greater or lesser extent, depending on regional accent. One frequently hears reference to the "purity" of vowels in European languages. By this "purity" is meant the absence of the diphthongal elements characteristic of some English vowels. Thus the pronunciation of the English word *Dane* [deɪn] is by no means the same as that for the German word *den* [deːn] "the."

Practice the contrast between English and German vowels in the following pairs of words. You will note that for the English diphthong sounds the jaw moves slightly during the pronunciation of the vowel. For the German sound, concentrate on holding the jaw in one position while articulating the vowel.

Exercise 6.1

Contrast:

English	German	
bate	Beet	"flowerbed"
lame	Lehm	"mud"

English	German	
lone	Lohn	"wage"
tote	tot	"dead"
toot	tut	"does"
geese	gieß	"pour"
puts	Putz	"finery"
bet	Bett	"bed"
pest	Pest	"pestilence"
mitt	mit	"with"
bin	bin	"am"

QUALITY

In Chapter 3, we discussed the distinction between closed, tense vowels and open, lax vowels. In German, except for the vowels *a* and *ä*, we can say that long vowels are *closed* and that short vowels are *open*. Thus the monophthongs discussed in this chapter—*i, ü* (and *y*), *e, ö, o, u*—will be long and closed in some positions and short and open in others.

LENGTH

In spoken German, a long vowel is actually extended to about double the duration of a short vowel. In singing, of course, the length of the vowel is largely determined by the length of the note on which it is sung. However, the composer usually assigns a longer note to a long vowel and a shorter note to a short vowel in order to reflect the difference in length of the spoken vowels.

In the IPA, length is indicated by a colon placed after the vowel, for example, [iː].

RULES ON LENGTH

The vowels of this chapter—*i, ü* (and *y*), *e, ö, o, u* (and only these vowels!)—may be either long and closed or short and open, depending on certain conditions[1]:

---

[1]The rules stated here also affect the *length* of *a* and *ä*; but since these two vowels do not follow the same pattern of qualitative distinction as the vowels of this chapter, they are treated elsewhere (see Chapter 9).

A. Long Vowels

The vowels of this chapter are regularly long and closed in the following positions:

1. before *h* [Normally, the *h* following a stressed vowel is not pronounced, even if it precedes another vowel (see also Chapter 13).]

Exercise 6.2   Pronounce:

1. stehlen	2. stehen
ihn	drohen
ohne	Ruhe
Ruhm	Flöhe
stöhnen	Brühe
rühren	

2. when doubled
Of the vowels in this chapter, only *ee* and *oo* occur doubled.[2]

Exercise 6.3   Pronounce:

Beet

Meer

Boot

Moor

3. before a single consonant

Exercise 6.4   Pronounce:

Reben	schuf
Weg	Muse
wider	öde
Boden	übel
bog	

B. Short Vowels

The monophthongs of this chapter are nearly always short and open when followed by more than one consonant.

Exercise 6.5   Pronounce:

denn	bunt
Ring	Hölle
Knospe	Lüfte

---

[2]The only other vowel that occurs doubled is *aa*, as in *Saal* [zɑːl] (see Chapter 9).

NOTES:

1. Exceptions

   There are common exceptions to the above rules on length. In particular, there are many words in which a vowel is pronounced long before *ch, st, r* + dental, and *ss* (or *ß*). In this book, the exceptions commonly found in song literature are listed under the discussion of each vowel. There are of course other exceptions to be found in Siebs; however, since none of these exceptions will appear in this book, it will not be necessary for the student to look up any word appearing in the exercises and excerpts once the rules and exceptions have been learned. Even in the large body of vocal literature beyond this text, it will be quite rare for the singer to encounter a word that does not conform to the rules and exceptions as outlined here.

2. *ß*: The *Eszett* or *scharfes s*

   The use of the character *ß* (called *Eszett* or *scharfes s*) is somewhat inconsistent in song texts. Sometimes it is not used at all, and the rules for its proper use are complicated and have changed from time to time. (See rules for the use of *ß* on page 96). Since *ß* in some instances appears in alternation with *ss*, since in some scores *ss* is used exclusively in place of *ß*, and since both *ß* and *ss* are always pronounced the same ([s]), we have elected to regard *ß* as a double consonant. This will explain the large number of apparent exceptions containing a long vowel before the *ß*.

3. Word Structure and Vowel Length

   In compound words, words with prefixes, and inflected words (those with grammatical endings), a basic knowledge of German word structure is necessary in order to recognize whether a vowel is followed by one consonant or more than one consonant. This subject is pursued in some detail in Chapter 7 and should be considered an integral part of these rules concerning length.

SECTION 1: *i*

[iː]

Long and closed [iː] is pronounced about like *i* in English *machine*. It occurs regularly before *h,* as in *ihn* [iːn] "him," or before a single consonant, as in *mir* [miːʁ] "me."

Exercise 6.6   Pronounce:

1. ihm, ihr, ihn, ihnen
2. wider, Titel, Bibel, Tiger
3. mir, wir, Appetit, Kredit

[ɪ]

Short and open [ɪ] is pronounced about like *i* in English *pick,* but higher in the mouth. It occurs regularly before two or more consonants as in *bist* [bɪst] "are."

Exercise 6.7   Pronounce:

1. bitte, spricht, ich, dich, Kind, ist, bist
2. Wirt, wird, irdisch, irgend, Kirsche, Kirche

Exceptions[3]

1. In certain words, *i* is short before a single consonant. Memorize these:

in, im	"in, in the"
bin	"am"
mit	"with"
hin	"there"
bis	"until"

2. In some suffixes ending in a single consonant, *i* is always short. Memorize these suffixes:

   -in

   -nis

   -ig (pronounced [ɪç])

Exercise 6.8   Pronounce:

1. Studentin	2. Ärgernis
Feindin	Kenntnis
Ärztin	Gefängnis
Berlinerin	3. fertig
Engländerin	giftig
	Käfig

3. In the final syllable *-ik, i* is long if the syllable is stressed and short if unstressed. Memorize the following:

Stressed	*Unstressed*
Musik	Chronik
Kritik	Tragik
Politik	Lyrik

[3]Many of the exceptions listed in this book may appear in various compounds; for example, *in* also appears in *darin, worin,* etc.—*mit* appears in *damit, mitgehen, mithin,* etc. Except as otherwise noted, the pronunciation of the basic word remains the same.

Exercise 6.9

Differentiate between [iː] and [ɪ] in the following pairs:

1. wider   Widder
2. Lid   litt
3. ihnen   innen
4. Stil   still
5. Mine   Minne
6. Iren   irren

Exercise 6.10

Pronounce the following words, applying the rules for long or short monophthongs:

1. Winter, sitzen, Igel, mir, Hirsch
2. finden, Stimme, ihn, in, bilden
3. Studentin, Bibel, Kenntnis, heilige, Mitte
4. April, Stil, Mine, hin, Titel
5. Musik, wider, Tragik, wissen, bin, mit

Exercise 6.11

Transcribe the above words into the IPA.

Excerpts

Read the following excerpts aloud, paying special attention to the pronunciation of *i:*

1. Doch bin ich, wie ich bin,
   Und nimm mich nur hin!
   Willst du bessre besitzen,
   So laß dir sie schnitzen.
   Ich bin nur, wie ich bin;
   So nimm mich nur hin.

   > *Liebhaber in allen Gestalten*
   > *Goethe/Schubert*

2. Seit ich ihn gesehen,
   Glaub' ich blind zu sein;
   Wo ich hin nur blicke,
   Seh' ich ihn allein.

   > *Frauenliebe und -leben*
   > *Chamisso/Schumann*

Song

Sing the following song, focusing on the contrast between [i] and [ɪ]. Note that *ie* is usually pronounced [iː].

Du, du, liegst mir im Herzen

Du,   du,   liegst mir im   Her - zen,   du,   du,
So,   so,   wie ich dich   lie - be,   so,   so,
Doch,   doch,   darf ich dir   trau - en, dir,   dir,
Und,   und,   wenn in der   Fer - ne   mir,   mir

liegst mir im   Sinn.   Du,   du,   machst mir viel Schmer-zen,
lie - be auch   mich.   Die,   die   zärt - lich-sten Trie - be
mit leich - tem Sinn?   Du,   du,   kannst auf mich bau - en,
dein Bild er - scheint,   dann,   dann,   wunscht' ich so   ger - ne,

weißt nicht wie gut ich dir bin. _____ Ja,   ja,
füh - le ich   ein - zig für dich. _____ Ja,   ja,
weißt ja wie   gut ich dir bin. _____ Ja,   ja,
daß uns die   Lie - be ver - eint. ____   Ja,   ja,

ja,	ja,	weißt nicht, wie	gut ich dir	bin. _____
ja,	ja,	füh - le ich	ein - zig für	dich. _____
ja,	ja,	weißt ja, wie	gut ich dir	bin. _____
ja,	ja,	daß uns die	Lie - be ver -	eint. _____

SECTION 2:   *ü, y*

The letter *ü* (also spelled *ue*) represents sounds which are variations of the sounds of *i*. The letter *y* follows the same rules for pronunciation as the letter *ü*.[4]

[y:]

Long and closed [y:] is the same sound as long and closed [i:] but is pronounced with the lips rounded. Pronounce an extended [i::::::] and, *without changing the position of the tongue or jaw,* slowly round the lips. Be aware that you are really pronouncing the sound [i:]. For both [i:] and [y:], the sides of the tongue are against the upper back molars, and the tip of the tongue rests in the lower jaw against the bottom of the teeth. Only the rounding of the lips makes the distinction between the two sounds. Practice alternating [i:] and [y:] by slowly rounding and unrounding the lips while pronouncing [i::::::].

The pronunciation of *ü* (or *y*) is regularly long and closed [y:] before *h*, as in *fühlen* ['fy:lən] "feel," or before a single consonant, as in *für* [fy:ʁ] "for," *Lyrik* ['ly:rɪk] "lyrics."

Exercise 6.12

Contrast the following pairs of words containing [i:] and [y:]:

1. Stile	Stühle
2. liegen	lügen
3. sieden	Süden
4. vier	für
5. Triebe	trübe
6. Miete	Mythe
7. Riemen	rühmen

[4]Except in some names and foreign words, for example, Fanny ['fani], York [jɔrk].

8. Fliege	Flüge
9. Biene	Bühne
10. Tier	Tür

Exercise 6.13   Pronounce only the words with *ü* in Exercise 6.12.

Exceptions

There are a few words in which *ü* is long before two or more consonants.[5] Memorize these:

1. before *st* in
Wüste	"desert"
düster	"somber"

2. before *ch* in
Bücher	"books"
Tücher	"cloths"

3. before *ß*[6] in
büßen	"atone"
müßig	"leisurely"
süß	"sweet"
grüßen	"greet"
Füße	"feet"

[ʏ]

Short and open [ʏ] is the same sound as short and open [ɪ] but is pronounced with the lips rounded. Pronounce an extended [ɪːːːːː] and, *without changing the position of the tongue or jaw,* slowly round the lips.

The position of the tongue is the same for both [ɪ] and [ʏ]. Only the rounding of the lips makes the distinction between the two sounds. Now practice alternating [ɪ] and [ʏ] by slowly rounding and unrounding the lips while pronouncing [ɪːːːːː].

Be aware that [iː] and [yː] are closed sounds and that [ɪ] and [ʏ] are open sounds; that is, the jaw is slightly dropped for the latter.

The pronunciation of *ü* and *y* is regularly short and open [ʏ] before two or more consonants, as in *fünf* [fʏnf] "five," *idyllisch* [iˈdʏlɪʃ] "idyllic."

Exercise 6.14   Contrast [ɪ] and [ʏ] in the following pairs of words:

1. Kissen	küssen
2. Kiste	Küste
3. sticken	Stücken
4. missen	müssen
5. Gericht	Gerücht
6. ticken	Tücken
7. Minze	Münze
8. Kinde	künde

[5]Normally, *ü* is short before *st, ch, ß,* as expected.

[6]See note on *ß,* p. 35.

Exercise 6.15   Pronounce only the words with *ü* in Exercise 6.14.

Exercise 6.16   Contrast long closed [y:] and short open [ʏ]:

1. Wüste   wüßte
2. fühle   fülle
3. rügte   rückte
4. Flüge   flügge
5. Hüte   Hütte
6. pflügte   pflückte
7. kühnste   Künste
8. büke   bücke

Exercise 6.17   Pronounce the following words, applying the rules for long or short monophthongs:

1. wütend, fühlen, Lyrik, Güte, Hülle, füttern
2. Münze, Walküre, dürfen, Hügel, flügge, Lüfte
3. Mythe, Hymne, Analyse, Küste, Wüste, typisch
4. düster, rüsten, fünf, fürchten, für, stürzen
5. müssen, büßen, süßen, wünschen, Jünger
6. dürrer, Dürer, würde, idyllisch, grün, Gründe
7. Frühling, Rhythmus, blühen, Schüssel, flüstern

Exercise 6.18   Transcribe the above words into the IPA.

Exercise 6.19   Read the following transcriptions aloud:

1. [bə'ry:mt, 'bry:dəʁ, 'by:nə, 'flʏçtɪç, 'bʏɾgəʁ]
2. ['dɾʏkən, 'dʏɾə, 'ky:çə, 'gɾy:sən, 'hy:tən]
3. [fɾy:, 'fʏtəʁn, 'fly:gəl, 'fʏlən, 'bly:tə]

Excerpts

1. Durch tote Wüsten wandle hin,
   Und grüne Schatten breiten sich,
   Ob fürchterliche Schwüle dort
   Ohn' Ende brüte, wonnevoll.
   Wie bist du, meine Königin
   Daumer/Brahms

2. Überm Garten durch die Lüfte
   Hör' ich Wandervögel zieh'n,
   Das bedeutet Frühlingsdüfte,
   Unten fängt's schon an zu blüh'n.
   Frühlingsnacht
   Eichendorff/Schumann

Song   Sing the following song, concentrating on the contrast between [y:] and [ʏ].

So sei gegrüßt viel tausendmal

So sei ge - grüßt viel tau - send - mal, hol - der, hol - der
Du kommst und froh ist al - le Welt, hol - der, hol - der
So sei ge - grüßt viel tau - send - mal, hol - der, hol - der

Früh - ling! Will - kom - men hier in un - serm Tal,
Früh - ling! Es freut sich Wie - se Wald und Feld,
Früh - ling! O bleib recht lang in un - serm Tal,

hol - der, hol - der Früh - ling! Hol - der Früh - ling ü - ber-all
hol - der, hol - der Früh - ling! Ju - bel tönt dir ü - ber-all,
hol - der, hol - der Früh - ling! Kehr in al - le Her - zen ein,

grü - ßen wir dich froh mit Sang und Schall, mit Sang und Schall.
dich be - grü - ßet Lerch und Nach - ti - gall, und Nach - ti - gall.
laß doch al - le mit uns fröh - lich sein, recht fröh - lich sein.

SECTION 3:   *e*

[eː]

Long and closed [eː] is basically the first element of the English diphthong [eɪ], as in *gate* [geɪt]. In pronouncing [eɪ], note how the sides of the tongue slide inward along the molars and how the tip of the tongue and the jaw rise slightly.

In articulating the German sound [eː], as in *geht* [geːt] "goes," all movement of the tongue and jaw, and hence all trace of the English diphthongal element [ɪ], must be avoided. First practice pronouncing an extended [eːːːːː], allowing no movement of tongue or jaw. Then practice pronouncing *geht,* exaggerating the length of the vowel [geːːːːːt] and allowing the tip of the tongue to rise only when articulating the [t].

The pronunciation of *e* is regularly long and closed [eː]: (1) when it occurs in a stressed syllable before *h,* as in *gehen* ['geːən] "go" (see also Chapter 13); (2) when it occurs doubled, as in *Beet* [beːt] "flowerbed"; and (3) when it occurs before a single consonant, as in *beten* ['beːtən] "pray."[7]

Exercise 6.20

Pronounce the following words containing [eː]:

1. Weh, stehlen, Sehnsucht, Ehre, Reh
2. Beet, Meer, Schnee, Klee, Fee
3. Weg, heben, legen, ewig, wer
4. den, dem, der, schwer, elend

Exceptions

In a few words, *e* is long before two or more consonants. Memorize the following:

1. followed by *r* + consonant (only in these words, otherwise short):

erst	"first"
Erde	"earth"
Herd	"hearth"
Schwert	"sword"
wert	"worth"
Beschwerde	"complaint"
Pferd	"horse"
werden	"become"
Erz	"metal"

---

[7]Since in conversational German the *e* is often pronounced short before *r* in words like *er, wer, der,* many singers tend to pronounce these words with [ɛ]. Since in these words *e* is followed by a single consonant, however, it should always be pronounced long: [eːʁ, veːʁ, deːʁ].

The word *Erz* "metal, ore" is pronounced with long [eː]. The syllable *Erz-* meaning "arch-" (as in "archangel," "archbishop," etc.) is pronounced, as expected, with short [ɛ].

2. followed by other consonants:

stets	"always"
Krebs	"crab, cancer"

[ɛ]

Short and open [ɛ] is approximately the same as the vowel sound in English *bet* but without any of the diphthongal elements typical of some accents in the United States.

Before two or more consonants *e* is usually short and open, as in *Bett* [bɛt] "bed."

Exercise 6.21   Pronounce the following words containing [ɛ]:

1. Held, Bett, Recht, Sessel, Stelle
2. stecken, gelb, denn, senden
3. Vers, Verse, Herz, Herzog, fertig

Exceptions

In a few instances, *e* is short before a single consonant. Memorize the following:

1. The short words:

es	"it"
des	"of the"
weg	"away"

The particle *weg* forms many compounds, for example *hinweg, weggehen,* in which the vowel is always pronounced [ɛ]. This contrasts with the noun *Weg* "way, path" and its compounds, e.g. *Wegweiser, Heimweg,* in which the vowel is always pronounced [eː].

2. The prefixes:

er-	as in *erkennen* "recognize"
ver-	as in *verlieren* "lose"
zer-	as in *zerstören* "destroy"

These prefixes are pronounced with short [ɛ] whether they are followed by a vowel or a consonant.

Exercise 6.22   Differentiate between [eː] and [ɛ] in the following pairs:

1. Heer   Herr
2. den   denn
3. wen   wenn
4. Kehle   Kelle
5. legte   leckte
6. zehren   zerren
7. fehl   Fell
8. Beet   Bett

Exercise 6.23   Pronounce the following words, applying the rules for the pronunciation of long and short vowels:

1. See, Nebel, ewig, essen, schelten, wehen
2. stehlen, Elend, hell, bersten, ersten
3. stets, des, wer, Weh, flehen, Weg
4. geben, weg, es, Herd, Werk, Lerche, lernen
5. Herz, Erzengel, Erde, dem, Epik

Exercise 6.24   Transcribe the above words into the IPA.

SECTION 3A: Unstressed e

Unstressed *e* is traditionally represented in reference works and textbooks as [ə]. In actual practice, singers regularly use [ə] only for final *e,* as in *bitte* [ˈbɪtə] "please," and *e* in some unstressed middle syllables; and even in these cases the *e* tends to be more open than in spoken German.

Exercise 6.25   Pronounce the following words containing [ə]:

1. rechte, Stelle, lasse, kämme, hebe
2. lege, schwere, stehle, Ehre
3. Taugenichts, liebevoll, bessere, bittere

In all other unstressed syllables, but specifically in the prefixes *ge-* and *be-,* the adjective endings *-es, -en, -em,* and the verb endings *-en, -et, -est,* singers tend to front the vowel somewhat, achieving a quality more akin to [ɛ] than to [ə]. However, since the references use [ə] in transcribing these syllables, this text will also follow this practice except for the prefixes *er-, ver-, zer-, emp-, ent-.* The voice student is urged to listen carefully to established singers to determine how much and in what position [ə] can be fronted.

It is important to note that unstressed *e* is not long and closed if followed by *h* or any other single consonant. Thus *gehangen* "hung" and *gegeben* "given" would be transcribed [gə'haŋən, gə'ge:bən].

The prefixes *er-*, *ver-*, *zer-*, *emp-*, *ent-*

In the prefixes *er-*, *ver-*, *zer-*, *emp-*, *ent-*, the *e* should always be pronounced and transcribed [ɛ], even though these syllables are almost always unstressed, as in *erfahren* [ɛɐ'fɑːrən] "experience," *vergessen* [fɛɐ'gɛsən] "forget."

Exercise 6.26

Pronounce the following words, paying special attention to the pronunciation of unstressed *e*:

1. gegeben, geehrt, begraben, beleben, geheimer
2. kühles, kühlen, kühlem
3. schweben, schwebest, schwebet

Exercise 6.27

Pronounce the following words, paying special attention to the pronunciation of unstressed *e*:

1. meine, meinen, meinem, Geliebte, Geliebten
2. stille, stilles, stillen, Garten, Sammetkleide
3. betend, werde, betreten, geteilt, betete

Exercise 6.28

Transcribe the words in Exercise 6.27 into the IPA.

Excerpts

Read the following excerpts aloud, paying special attention to the pronunciation of unstressed *e*:

1. Dem Schnee, dem Regen,
   Dem Wind entgegen,
   Im Dampf der Klüfte,
   Durch Nebeldüfte.
      Rastlose Liebe
      Goethe/Schubert

2. Wer trägt der Himmel unzählbare Sterne?
   Wer führt die Sonn' aus ihrem Zelt?
   Sie kommt und leuchtet und lacht uns von ferne
   Und läuft den Weg gleich als ein Held.

   Kannst du der Wesen unzählbare Heere,
   Den kleinsten Staub fühllos beschaun?
   Durch wen ist alles? O gib ihm die Ehre!
   "Mir," ruft der Herr, "sollst du vertraun."
      Die Ehre Gottes aus der Natur
      Gellert/C.P.E. Bach

Song

Sing the following song, paying special attention to all *es*, accented and unaccented.

Guten Abend, gut' Nacht

Gu - ten A - bend, gut' Nacht, mit__ Ro - sen be -
dacht,__ mit__ Näg - lein be - steckt, schlupf un - ter die
Deck'. Mor - gen früh, wenn Gott will, wirst du wie - der ge -
weckt,__ mor - gen früh, wenn Gott will, wirst du wie - der ge - weckt.

Gu - ten A - bend, gut' Nacht, von__ Eng - lein be -
wacht,__ die__ zei - gen im__ Traum dir__ Christ - kind - leins
Baum. Schlaf nun se - lig und süß, schau im Traum's Pa - ra -
dies,__ schlaf nun se - lig und süß, schau im Traum's Pa - ra - dies.

SECTION 4:   *ö*

The letter *ö* (also spelled *oe*) represents sounds which are variations of the sounds of *e*.

[ø:]

Long and closed [ø:] is the same sound as long and closed [e:] but is pronounced with the lips rounded. Pronounce an extended [e:::::] and, *without changing the position of the tongue or jaw,* slowly round the lips. Be aware that you are really pronouncing the sound [e:]. Keep the sides of the tongue against the upper molars and the tip of the tongue against the base of the lower teeth; now, practice alternating [e:] and [ø:] by slowly rounding and unrounding the lips while pronouncing [e:::::].

The pronunciation of *ö* is regularly long and closed [ø:] before *h*, as in *fröhlich* ['frø:lɪç] "merry," and before a single consonant, as in *schön* [ʃø:n] "lovely."

Exercise 6.29   Contrast [e:] and [ø:] in the following pairs of words:

1.	Meere	Möhre
2.	Lehne	Löhne
3.	lesen	lösen
4.	Besen	bösen
5.	verheeren	verhören
6.	flehe	Flöhe
7.	beten	böten
8.	hebe	höbe
9.	hehlen	Höhlen
10.	sehne	Söhne

Exercise 6.30   Pronounce only the words with *ö* in Exercise 6.29.

Exceptions

There are a few words in which *ö* is pronounced long before two or more consonants.[8] Memorize these:

1. before *ß*[9] in

Größe	"greatness"
größer-, größt-	"greater, greatest"
Blöße	"bareness"
stößt	"pushes"

[8]Normally, *ö* is short before *st, ch, ß,* as expected.
[9]See note on *ß,* p. 35.

2. before *st* in

trösten	"console"
rösten	"roast"

3. before *ch* in

höchst [høːçst]	"highest"

[œ]

Short and open [œ] is the same as short and open [ɛ] but is pronounced with the lips rounded. Pronounce an extended [ɛːːːːː] and, *without changing the position of the tongue or jaw,* slowly round the lips but not as much as for [øː]. Remember that [eː] and [øː] are both closed sounds and [ɛ] and [œ] are both open sounds.

Now practice alternating [ɛ] and [œ] by slowly rounding and unrounding the lips while pronouncing [ɛːːːːː]. The pronunciation of *ö* is regularly short and open [œ] before two or more consonants, as in *könnte* ['kœntə] "could."

Exercise 6.31

Contrast [ɛ] and [œ] in the following pairs:

1. Mächte	möchte
2. stecke	Stöcke
3. helle	Hölle
4. Kellner	Kölner
5. fällig	völlig
6. fechte	föchte
7. Schwämme	schwömme
8. kernig	körnig

Exercise 6.32

Pronounce only the words with *ö* in Exercise 6.31.

Exercise 6.33

Contrast [øː] and [œ] in the following pairs:

1. Höhle	Hölle
2. gewöhnen	gewönnen
3. Söhne	sönne
4. Höker	Höcker
5. Schöße	schösse
6. blöken	Blöcken

Exercise 6.34

Pronounce the following words, applying the rules for long and short monophthongs:

1. versöhnen, böse, möchte, östlich, Getöse
2. öde, Töchter, plötzlich, töten, Schöpfer
3. nötig, Erlkönig, größte, schön, trösten

4. köstlich, höchstens, Dörflein, Blöße, schösse

5. höher, fröhlich, Löcher, völlig, könnte

Exercise 6.35   Transcribe the above examples into the IPA.

Exercise 6.36   Read the following transcriptions aloud:

1. ['hø:ɾən, 'ʃtø:nən, 'lœʃən, 'tø:nə, gœnt]

2. [de:n, 'e:dəl, 'lø:zən, dɛn, 'fe:ləʁ, 'ly:ɾɪʃ]

3. ['hɛftɪçstən, 'œfnən, 'lø:və, gə'be:t, ve:ʁ]

4. [i'de:, 'gœtəʁ, 'kœɾpəʁ, ɪn'de:m, hɪn'vɛk]

5. ['plœtslɪç, mœnç, bə'daχt, 'flɛçtən, 'tø:tlɪç]

Excerpts   Read the following excerpts aloud, concentrating on the pronunciation of *ö*:

1. Kömmt mir der Tag in die Gedanken,
   Möcht' ich noch einmal rückwärts sehn,
   Möcht' ich zurücke wieder wanken,
   Vor ihrem Hause stille stehn.
   Die Winterreise
   Müller/Schubert

2. Will dich im Traum nicht stören,
   Wär' schad' um deine Ruh',
   Sollst meinen Tritt nicht hören—
   Sacht, sacht die Türe zu!
   Die Winterreise
   Müller/Schubert

Song   Sing the following song, concentrating on the pronunciation of *ö*.

Heidenröslein

Hei - den,   war   so   jung   und   mor - gen - schön,   lief   er   schnell, es
Hei - den!"   Rös - lein sprach: "Ich   ste - che dich,   daß   du   e - wig
Hei - den,   Rös - lein wehr - te   sich   und stach,   half   ihm doch— kein

nah   zu sehn,   sah's   mit   vie - len   Freu - den.   Rös - lein,   Rös - lein
denkst an mich,   und   ich   will's—   nicht   lei - den."   Rös - lein,   Rös - lein
Weh   und Ach,   mußt' es   e - ben   lei - den.   Rös - lein,   Rös - lein

Rös - lein   rot,   Rös - lein   auf   der   Hei - den!
Rös - lein   rot,   Rös - lein   auf   der   Hei - den!
Rös - lein   rot,   Rös - lein   auf   der   Hei - den!

SECTION 5:   *o*

[oː]

Long and closed [oː] is similar to the initial element in the English diphthong
[oʊ], as in *lone* [loʊn]. In pronouncing [oʊ], note how the jaw and the tip of
the tongue rise slightly for the second part of the diphthong.

In articulating the German sound [oː], as in *Lohn* [loːn] "wage," all movement of the tongue and jaw, and hence all trace of the English diphthongal element [ʊ], must be avoided. First practice pronouncing an extended [oːːːːː], allowing no movement of the tongue or jaw. Then practice pronouncing *Lohn,* exaggerating the length of the vowel—[loːːːːːn]—and allowing the tip of the tongue to rise only when articulating the [n].

The pronunciation of *o* is regularly long and closed [oː]: (1) when it occurs in a stressed syllable before *h,* as in *ohne* ['oːnə] "without"; (2) when it occurs doubled, as in *Boot* [boːt] "boat"; and (3) when it occurs before a single consonant, as in *schon* [ʃoːn] "already".

Exercise 6.37   Pronounce the following words containing long *o*:

  1. ohne, Sohle, Lohn, froh, empfohlen, Kohle

  2. Boot, Moos, Moor

  3. Boden, holen, Monat, Vogel, Not, Los

  4. Hof, Ton, rot, schon, Tor, Tod, vor

Exceptions

In a number of words, *o* is long and closed before two or more consonants.[10] Memorize the following:

1. *hoch* "high" and its many compounds, for example

    hocherfreut

    Hochgefühl

    hochbegabt

(Note, however, that *o* is short and open in *Hochzeit* "wedding"!)

2. before *st* in:

Ostern	"Easter"
Kloster	"cloister"
prost	"to your health!" (a toast)
Trost	"solace"
getrost	"confident"

3. before *ß*[11] in

bloß	"bare, simply"
Schoß	"bosom, lap"
groß	"large, great"
stoßen	"push"

---

[10]Normally, *o* is short before *ch, st, ß,* as expected.

[11]See note on *ß*, p. 35.

4. other words

Mond	"moon"
Montag	"Monday"
Obst	"fruit"
Vogt	"warden, governor"

[ɔ]

Short and open [ɔ] is similar to the English sound represented by the same symbol, but it is usually much shorter and slightly more open. It is very much like the *o* sound in the British pronunciation of the word *hot*. The articulation of [ɔ] is similar to that for [o] but is further back.

Short [ɔ] occurs regularly before two or more consonants, as in *doch* [dɔχ] "but."

Exercise 6.38   Pronounce the following words containing short *o*:

1. hoffen, kommen, wollen, fordern, Sporn, Rock
2. Sommer, Sonne, Wolke, voll, folgen, Schopf
3. stolz, Stock, Bock, dort, fort, Holz
4. Frosch, Groschen, doch, noch, Joch, Woche

Exceptions

In a few words, *o* is short and open before a single consonant. Memorize the following:

ob	"whether"
von, vom	"of, of the"

Exercise 6.39   Contrast [oː] and [ɔ] in the following pairs:

1. Gote	Gotte
2. wohne	Wonne
3. Tone	Tonne
4. bog	Bock
5. Wohle	Wolle
6. bohrte	Borte
7. Hofe	hoffe
8. Ofen	offen

Exercise 6.40   Pronounce the following words containing *o,* following the rules for long and short monophthongs:

1. Vogel, stolz, ohne, drohen, Tonne, mochte
2. Stoff, Mond, Dolch, Sonne, Sohn
3. hoch, Kloster, kosten, Trost, Posten, Ostern, Osten, Hochschule
4. Schoß, schoß, Schloß, großen, Roß, bloße

5. Horizont, Obst, ob, Ton, von, vom, Dom

6. Hochzeit, Wollust, gestoßen, gegossen, Gold

7. empor, Bischof, Kleinod, Komik, davon, frohlocken

Exercise 6.41   Transcribe the words in Exercise 6.40 into the IPA.

Excerpts   Read the following excerpts aloud, paying careful attention to the pronunciation of *o*:

1. Als müßte in dem Garten,
   Voll Rosen weiß und rot,
   Meine Liebste auf mich warten,
   Und ist doch lange tot.
   > *Erinnerung*
   > *Eichendorff/Schumann*

2. Alles nimmt sie, was nur hold,
   Nimmt das Silber weg des Stroms,
   Nimmt vom Kupferdach des Doms
   Weg das Gold.
   > *Die Nacht*
   > *Gilm/Strauß*

Song   Sing the following two songs, concentrating on the pronunciation of *o*.

Lili Marleen

Vor der Ka-ser-ne   vor dem gro-ßen Tor   stand 'ne La-ter-ne und
Uns-re bei-den Schat-ten   sah'n wie ei-ner aus; daß   wir so lieb uns hat-ten, das
Schon rief der Po-sten:"sie   bla-sen Zap-fen-streich,   es kann drei Tage ko-sten;"Kam'-
Dei-ne Schritte kennt sie,   dei-nen zie-ren Gang,   al-le A-bend brennt sie, doch

steht sie noch da-vor,   so woll'n wir da uns   wie-der-sehn, bei
sah man gleich dar-aus.   Und al-le Leu-te   soll'n es sehn, wenn
rad, ich kom-me gleich.   Da sag-ten wir "Auf Wie-der-sehn," wie
mich ver-gaß sie lang.   Und soll-te mir ein Leid ge-schehn, wer

der   La - ter - ne woll'n wir stehn, wie einst, Li - li Mar -
wir   bei der   La - ter - ne stehn, wie einst, Li - li Mar -
ger - ne   wollt' ich mit dir gehn, wie einst, Li - li Mar -
wird   bei der   La - ter - ne stehn, mit dir, Li - li Mar -

leen,   wie   einst,   Li - li   Mar - leen.
leen,   wie   einst,   Li - li   Mar - leen.
leen,   wie   einst,   Li - li   Mar - leen.
leen,   mit   dir,   Li - li   Mar - leen.

O wie wohl ist mir am Abend

(Canon)

O   wie wohl ist   mir am A - bend, mir am A - bend, wenn zur Ruh die

Glok - ken läu - ten, Glok - ken läu - ten, bim, bam,   bim, bam, bim, bam!

SECTION 6:   *u*

[uː]

German long and closed [uː] is similar to the English vowel in *moot*. For German [uː], as in *Mut,* the lips are somewhat more protruded and somewhat more rounded than for the English sound. Long and closed [uː] occurs regularly before *h,* as in *Ruhe* [ˈɾuːə] "rest," or before a single consonant, as in *Flut* [fluːt] "flood."

Exercise 6.42

Pronounce the following words containing [uː]:

1. Kuh, Schuh, Huhn, Buhle, Uhr, Stuhl, Ruhe
2. rufen, gut, nun, schuf, Flug, Schule, Dur

Exceptions

In a number of words, *u* is long before two or more consonants.[12] Memorize the following:

1. before *ß*[13] in

Buße	"atonement"
Fuß	"foot"
Gruß	"greeting"
Muße	"leisure"

2. before *ch* in

Buch	"book"
Tuch	"cloth"
ruchlos	"wicked"
suchen	"seek"
Fluch	"curse"
Kuchen	"cake"

3. before *st* in

Schuster	"shoemaker"
husten	"cough"

4. also in

Geburt	"birth"

---

[12]Normally, *u* is short before *ß, ch, st,* as expected.

[13]See note on *ß,* p. 35.

[ʊ]

German short and open [ʊ] is very similar to the vowel sound in English *puts*. It occurs regularly before two or more consonants, as in *Putz* [pʊts] "finery."

Exercise 6.43   Pronounce the following words containing [ʊ]:

1. Putz, Wunder, Kunst, Kupfer, Busch
2. Schutz, Luft, Druck, nutzen, bunt
3. Wunsch, gesund, Götterfunken, Puppe, dumm
4. muß, Fluß, Frucht, Flucht, wußte

Exceptions

There are a few words in which *u* is short before a single consonant. Memorize the following:

um	"around" (also a prefix)
un-	prefix meaning "*un-*"
zum	"to the" (however, *u* is long in *zu* "to")
Jesus	"Jesus"
Rum	"rum"

Exercise 6.44   Contrast [uː] and [ʊ] in the following pairs:

1. Mus   muß
2. Muhme   Mumme
3. schuft   Schuft
4. Ruhm   Rum
5. sucht   Sucht
6. spuken   spucken
7. Stuhle   Stulle
8. Buhle   Bulle
9. bucht   Bucht
10. flucht   Flucht
11. Flugs   flugs

Exercise 6.45   Pronounce the following words containing *u,* applying the rules for long and short monophthongs:

1. Flut, Mutter, Bube, du, rufen, Kunst
2. Luft, Lust, Puls, Kurs, Kur, Kultur, hundert
3. Umsturz, Bucht, Buch, Kuß, Fluß, Fuß
4. Brusttuch, Schuster, Muster, Demut, Fluch, fluchen
5. Blut, Armut, Bruch, Schuß, lustig, Brust, Jesus

6. Kutsche, jung, genug, gute, Geduld, Druck

7. Wurzel, bewundern, Mund, Bursche, Genuß

Exercise 6.46   Transcribe the above words into the IPA.

Exercise 6.47   Read the following transcriptions aloud:

A. 1. [ˈbuːlə, fluːk, zuːχt, fɾʊχt, hʊlt, jʊχˈheː]
   2. [gɾoːp, ˈhoːnɪç, noːt, ˈzɔndɐʁn, aˈpɔstəl, zɔlç]
   3. [ɛʁˈlɔʃən, gəˈnɔsən, gʊnst, fɐʁˈfluːχt, ˈbuːzən]

B. Note: [|] represents a glottal stop (see Chapter 7).
[zeː |ɪç ziː |am ˈbaχə ˈzɪtsən
vɛn ziː ˈfliːgən͵netsə ʃtɾɪkt
ˈoːdɐʁ ˈzɔntaːks fyːʁ di ˈfɛnstɐʁ
ˈfɾɪʃə ˈviːzən͵bluːmən pflʏkt

zeː |ɪç ziː tsʊm ˈgaɾtən ˈvandəln
mɪt deːm ˈkœɾpçən |ɪn deːʁ hant
naːχ deːn ˈeːɾstən ˈbeːɾən ˈʃpeːən
an deːʁ ˈgɾyːnən ˈdɔɾnən͵vant]

Excerpts   Read the following excerpts aloud, paying special attention to the pronunciation of *u*:

1. Herzeleid und viel Verdruß—
   Eine Schul' und enge Mauern,—
   Carreaukönig, der bedauern,
   Und zuletzt mich trösten muß.—
   Ein Geschenk auf art'ge Weise—
   Er entführt mich—Eine Reise—
   Geld und Lust im Überfluß!
   Die Kartenlegerin
   Chamisso/Schumann

2. Und du singst, was ich gesungen,
   Was mir aus der vollen Brust
   Ohne Kunstgepräng' erklungen,
   Nur der Sehnsucht sich bewußt.
   An die ferne Geliebte
   Jeitteles/Beethoven

Tape   Practice reading the lyrics of the following song. Then read them onto a tape without stopping the recorder.

Song   Sing the following song, concentrating on the pronunciation of *u*.

Die Lorelei

Ich weiß nicht, was soll es be - deu - ten, daß ich so trau - rig
Die schön - ste Jung - frau sit - zet dort o - ben wun - der -
Den Schif - fer im klei - nen Schif - fe er - greift es mit wil - dem

bin;____ ein Mär - chen aus al - ten Zei - ten, das
bar;____ ihr gold' - nes Ge - schmei - de blit - zet, sie
Weh;____ er schaut nicht die Fel - sen - rif - fe, er

kommt mir nicht aus dem Sinn.____ Die Luft ____ ist kühl und es
kämmt ihr gol - de - nes Haar.____ Sie kämmt es mit gol - de - nem
schaut nur hin - auf in die Höh'.____ Ich glau - be die Wel - len ver -

dun - kelt   und   ru - hig   fließt ____ der   Rhein; _____ der
Kam - me   und   singt   ein   Lied ____ da - bei, _____ das
schlin - gen   am   En - de   Schif - fer   und   Kahn_____ und

Gip - fel des Ber - ges fun - kelt im A - bend - son - nen - schein.____
hat ei - ne wun - der - sa - me ge - walt' - ge Me - lo - dei.____
das hat mit ih - rem Sin - gen die Lo - re - lei____ ge - tan.____

7 Word Structure

SECTION 1: STRUCTURAL ELEMENTS

There are certain problems of pronunciation that can be resolved only through a knowledge of German word structure. These problems require identification of four main types of structural elements: A. prefixes; B. suffixes; C. parts of compound words; D. inflectional endings. Perhaps surprisingly, the rules for syllable division in simple words do not provide significant information in determining pronunciation.[1]

A. Prefixes[2]

The following is a list of common German prefixes. You will recall that several prefixes do not conform to the rules of pronunciation; transcriptions of these prefixes are provided.

ab- [ap]	abreisen	[ˈapˌraezən]	"depart"
an- [an]	ankommen	[ˈanˌkɔmən]	"arrive"
auf-	aufsehen	[ˈaofˌzeːən]	"look up"

---

[1]Although the rules for syllable division in simple words do not provide significant help in determining pronunciation, they are outlined below for the singer's information since every musical score contains words that are divided into syllables to be sung on different notes.

1. Division falls before a single consonant: *ge-ben, Frie-den.* Since *ch, sch, ß, ph,* and *th* represent single sounds, the syllable division falls before them: *Be-cher, lö-schen, Stra-ße, Te-le-phon, A-po-the-ke.*
2. Division falls before the final consonant of a cluster: *kämp-fen, hol-der, sen-den.* The combination *ck* is written *k-k* when divided: *blik-ken = blicken.*
3. Although in simple words double consonants represent single sounds, they are separated in syllable division: *ret-ten, Was-ser, hel-le.*
4. The combination *st,* although it represents two sounds, is never separated in simple words: *be-ste, Mei-ster.*

[2]Since the prefixes and suffixes listed here can have a significant effect on the pronunciation of a word, they should be learned for recognition.

aus-	ausruhen	['aos͜ruːən]	"rest"
be- [bə]	beglücken	[bə'glʏkən]	"make happy"
bei-	Beifall	['bae͜fal]	"applause"
da-	dafür	[da'fyːʁ]	"for it"
dar-	Darstellung	['daːɾ͜ʃtɛlʊŋ]	"performance"
durch-	durchspielen	['dʊrç͜ʃpiːlən]	"play through"
ein-	einsingen	['aen͜zɪŋən]	"practice singing"
ent- [ɛnt]	entlaufen	[ɛnt'laofən]	"run away"
er- [ɛʁ]	erfüllen	[ɛʁ'fʏlən]	"fulfill"
fort-	fortlaufen	['fɔrt͜laofən]	"run away"
ge- [gə]	gesehen	[gə'zeːən]	"seen"
her-[3]	herkommen	['heːʁ͜kɔmən]	"come here"
hin- [hɪn]	hingehen	['hɪn͜geːən]	"go there"
miß-	mißtrauen	[mɪs'traoen]	"mistrust"
mit- [mɪt]	mitgehen	['mɪt͜geːən]	"go along"
nach- [naːχ]	nacheilen	['naːχ͜aelən]	"hurry after"
über-	überfluten	[yːbəʁ'fluːtən]	"overflow"
um- [ʊm]	Umweg	['ʊm͜veːk]	"detour"
un- [ʊn]	unglücklich	['ʊn͜glʏklɪç]	"unhappy"
unter-	unterirdisch	['ʊntəʁ͜ɪrdɪʃ]	"subterranean"
ur-	uralt	['uːɾ͜alt]	"ancient"
ver- [fɛʁ]	vergolden	[fɛʁ'gɔldən]	"gild"
vor-	Vorsicht	['foːʁ͜zɪçt]	"caution"
weg- [vɛk]	weggehen	['vɛk͜geːən]	"go away"
zer- [tsɛʁ]	zerreißen	[tsɛʁ'raesən]	"tear up"
zu-	zueilen	['tsuː͜aelən]	"hurry to"

The pronunciation of each prefix is constant regardless of what follows it, since a prefix always constitutes a separate structural element in a word.

B. Suffixes

The most common German suffixes are:

-bar	trinkbar	['trɪŋkbaːr]	"drinkable"
-chen	Männchen	['mɛnçən]	"little man"
-haft	mannhaft	['manhaft]	"manly"

---

[3]When *her-* is unstressed, as in *hervor* [hɛʁ'foːʁ] "forth," it is pronounced [hɛʁ]; when it is stressed, as in *herkommen* ['heːʁ͜kɔmən] "come here" or when it stands alone, it is pronounced [heːʁ].

-heit	Kindheit	['kɪnthaet]	"childhood"
-keit	Göttlichkeit	['gœtlɪçkaet]	"godliness"
-lein	Männlein	['mɛnlaen]	"little man"
-lich	freundlich	['frɔøntlɪç]	"friendly"
-los	herzlos	['hɛrtsloːs]	"heartless"
-nis [nɪs]	Finsternis	['fɪnstɐʁnɪs]	"darkness"
-sal	Trübsal	['tryːpzɑːl]	"sorrow"
-sam	wachsam	['vaχzɑːm]	"wakeful"
-schaft	Landschaft	['lantʃaft]	"landscape"
-tum	Reichtum	['raeçtuːm]	"wealth"

C. Compound Words

German is well known for its many compound words, such as *Waldeinsamkeit* and *Meistersinger.* In many instances, the singer must be able to break the words into their component elements in order to pronounce them correctly. Some words are simply put together, such as *Meistersinger.* Others are joined with a connective element. It is helpful to be able to recognize the four common connective elements: (1) *e,* as in *Hundehütte*; (2) *(e)n,* as in *Rosenblatt*; (3) *er,* as in *Kindergarten*; (4) *(e)s,* as in *Liebestraum.* Fortunately, it is usually apparent how compounds should be divided; however, for some words, the singer must have some knowledge of German in order to decide pronunciation questions such as unvoicing or division of consonant clusters.

D. Inflectional Endings

Frequently, the singer needs to have a knowledge of inflection, especially verb inflection, in order to resolve questions concerning pronunciation.

Below are parts of a model verb, *legen,* "to lay," which will be used to illustrate certain pronunciation problems.

Present tense:

ich lege	"I lay," etc.	wir legen
du legst		ihr legt
er, sie, es legt		sie legen

Past tense:

ich legte	"I laid," etc.	wir legten
du legtest		ihr legtet
er, sie, es legte		sie legten

Past participle:

gelegt   "laid," as in "I have *laid*"

Another ending which the student should be able to recognize is the genitive singular *s* of nouns, as in *Betrugs,* genitive of *Betrug* "betrayal."

SECTION 2: *PRONUNCIATION PROBLEMS*

There are four main types of pronunciation problems that may require a knowledge of the structural elements: I. vowel length; II. unvoicing; III. consonant clusters; IV. the glottal stop.

I. Vowel Length

In Chapter 6, it was pointed out that a vowel followed by a single consonant is usually long.[4] In compounds and inflected forms, vowels which are *apparently* followed by two or more consonants are often long. The words must be broken down into structural elements in order to determine whether the vowel is in fact followed by a single consonant or more than one consonant.

A. Prefixes

In general, the pronunciation of a prefix remains the same, regardless of what follows it. Thus the vowel in *vor-* is long whether the prefix is followed by a vowel or a consonant: *Voreltern* ['foːʁ|ɛltəʁn] "ancestors," *Vorvater* ['foːʁˌfɑːtəʁ] "forefather."

A number of prefixes are pronounced with a short vowel even though they end with a single consonant (see list under "Prefixes" above and Chapter 6); this pronunciation is not affected by what follows the prefix. Thus the vowel in *mit* is short whether the prefix is followed by a vowel or a consonant: *mitessen* ['mɪtˌɛsən] "dine with," *mitgehen* ['mɪtˌgeːən] "go along."

B. Suffixes

If a single consonant stands between a vowel and a suffix, as in *Rös-lein,* then the vowel is long: ['ʁøːslaen].

Exercise 7.1   Pronounce the following words:

1. lesbar, Blümchen, boshaft, Bosheit, Röslein
2. tödlich, tonlos, Verlöbnis, Trübsal, strebsam, Botschaft

---

[4]Recall that the vowels treated in Chapter 6 are closed as well as long when they occur before a single consonant.

C. Compounds

If a compound divides so that a vowel is followed by a single consonant as in *Betbuch* "prayer book," then the vowel is long: ['beːtˌbuːχ].

Exercise 7.2

Pronounce the following compounds:

1. Bluttat, demselben, Flughafen, Lebtag
2. Lobgesang, Blutgeld, losgeben, fürwahr, Hofleute
3. jedweder, Rotkäppchen, totschlagen, Fluggast
4. Gutteil, Betstunde, Brotherr, Wegweiser, Tonkunst

D. Inflection

If a verb has a long vowel in the infinitive, then this vowel will normally be pronounced long regardless of inflectional endings.

Infinitive:

legen   ['leːgən]

Present tense:

du legst   [leːkst]
er legt   [leːkt]
etc.

Past tense:

ich legte   ['leːktə]
etc.

Past participle:

gelegt   [gə'leːkt]

Likewise, if a noun has a long vowel, the presence of an inflectional ending will not affect the quality of the vowel.

Nominative:

Betrug   [bə'truːk]

Genitive:

Betrugs   [bə'truːks]

Words ending in *-el, -en,* and *-er* often lose the *e* when adding inflectional endings or suffixes. (Use the name *Eleanor* to remember these syllables.) This does not affect the length of a preceding vowel (see also next section "Unvoicing").

edel ['eːdəl]	edle ['eːdlə]
Ekel ['eːkəl]	eklig ['eːklɪç]
wider ['viːdəʁ]	widrig ['viːdrɪç]

Exercise 7.3

Pronounce the following words containing inflectional endings:

1. lebst, bewegt, verlobt, klebt, Bahnhofs
2. verflucht, beschwört, beschert, gegrüßt, getönt
3. betont, Berufs, tobst, gelöst
4. grünst, büßte, hegte, lebtest

II. Unvoicing

The consonants *b, d, g,* and *s*[5] are pronounced as their voiceless equivalents [p, t, k, s] when they occur: (1) at the end of a word, as in *Bad* [baːt] "bath"; (2) before a consonant, as in *Magd* [maːkt] "maid"; and (3) at the end of an element in a compound, as in *Abendessen* ['aːbəntˌɛsən] "supper."

Exercise 7.4

Pronounce the following:

Tag	Vogt
Bad	Abt
Mond	beredt
leb'	

A. Prefixes

The only important prefix ending in one of these consonants is *ab-*. It is always pronounced [ap], as in *abändern* ['apˌɛndəʁn] "transform," *ablegen* ['apˌleːgən] "take off." The singer is cautioned about words such as *aber* ['aːbəʁ] "but" and *Abend* ['aːbənt] "evening," in which *ab* is not a prefix.

Exercise 7.5

Pronounce the following:

ablegen	aberkennen
abspielen	Aberglaube
abgeneigt	Abendmahl

---

[5]The consonant *v* is also affected to some extent by these rules (see Chapter 16), *w* is only rarely affected.

B. Suffixes

Since a number of suffixes begin with consonants, *b, d, g,* and *s* will be unvoiced before them, as in *freundlich, endlos, Wildnis, strebsam,* and *lesbar.* However, this does not really represent a special case of the general rule, which states simply that *b, d, g,* and *s* are unvoiced before consonants.

When *b, d, g,* and *s* occur before *l, n,* and *r* in inflected forms and derivatives of words ending in *-el, -en,* or *-er,* they are *not* usually unvoiced. (Remember *Eleanor!*) It will not always be easy for the singer with only a passing knowledge of German to recognize such forms. A number of examples are listed in Exercise 7.6 below to provide some familiarity with the type. Recall from the previous section ("Vowel Length") that long vowels remain long in inflected forms and derivatives such as *edle* ['eːdlə], *ebne* ['eːbnə].

Exercise 7.6

Pronounce the following words paying special attention to *b, d, g, s*:

1. siedle (< siedeln)
2. Siedlung (< siedeln)
3. edle (< edel)
4. Adlige (< Adel)
5. Adler (< Adel)
6. ebne (< eben)
7. übler (< übel)
8. goldne (< golden)
9. handle (< handeln)
10. eigner (< eigen)
11. andre (< ander)
12. seidnes (< seiden)
13. Wandrer (< wandern)
14. Wagner (< Wagen)
15. Wandlung (< wandeln)
16. Bogner (< Bogen)
17. regnet (< Regen)
18. irdne (< irden)
19. Redner (< reden)
20. Ordnung (< older form *ordenung*)
21. unsre (< unser)
22. heisrem (< heiser)
23. Gegner (< gegen)
24. Lügner (< lügen)

C. Compounds

If an element in a compound ends in *b, d, g,* or *s* and is followed by an element beginning with a consonant, as in *Mondschein* "moonlight" or *Diebstahl* "theft," the final *b, d, g,* or *s* in that element is of course unvoiced: ['moːntʃaen, 'diːpʃtaːl]. The singer does not really have to be able to separate the elements, since *b, d, g, s* are unvoiced before any consonant.

If, however, the second element begins with a vowel, the singer must be able to break down the word in order to know that the consonant is at the end of the first element and unvoiced rather than at the beginning of the second element and voiced. In *Lesart* ['leːs|aːrt] "version" and *Blasinstrument* ['blaːs|ɪnstruˌment] "wind instrument," for example, it is important to recognize that *s* belongs to the first element and is pronounced [s]; if it belonged to the second element, it would be pronounced [z].

Exercise 7.7   Pronounce the following:

1. Lobgesang	6. Argwohn
2. Abendsonne	7. Abendessen
3. bergab	8. bandartig
4. bergauf	9. Bergsteiger
5. endgültig	10. Bildhauer

D. Inflection

If a voiced consonant appears before an ending beginning with a consonant, then it of course becomes unvoiced: *legst* [leːkst], *legt* [leːkt], *gelegt* [gəˈleːkt], *Betrugs* [bəˈtruːks]. It will not be unvoiced before an ending beginning with a vowel: *legest* [ˈleːgəst].

It frequently happens that an inflectional ending is dropped in a song text, reflecting common spoken practice: *hab' ich* instead of *habe ich*. Strictly speaking, the final consonant in such a case should become unvoiced: [haːp ɪç], and indeed many singers use this articulation. However, many singers prefer to maintain the voicing as if the *e* ending were still there: [haːb ɪç]. Unfortunately, scores do not consistently use the apostrophe to indicate that an ending has been dropped.

III. Consonant Clusters

Certain combinations of consonants have a particular pronunciation when they appear together in a simple word. If, however, the same consonants appear together but belong to different elements in a word, they must be pronounced not as a unit but as parts of the separate elements.

For example, *sch* is pronounced [ʃ] in a simple word such as *löschen* [ˈlœʃən] "extinguish." If, however, *s* and *ch* come together as parts of two different elements, as they do in *Röschen* "little rose," then this must be reflected in the pronunciation: [ˈrøːsçən].

In simple words, double consonants are usually pronounced the same as single consonants, for example, in *Betten* [ˈbɛtən] "beds." If, on the other hand, the double consonant represents parts of two elements, as in *Bettag* "day of prayer," the pronunciation of the *t* is lengthened: [ˈbeːtˌtaːk].

The following consonant clusters occur frequently in German:

bl	br
	dr
fl	fr
gl	gr
kl	kr

pl   pr

          tr

schl   schr   schm   schn

If one of the above clusters occurs in one element, it is called a *blend* and is pronounced as a single unit. If, however, part of such a combination belongs to one element and part to another, each part of the combination is pronounced with its respective element. Contrast for example *zugleich (zu + gleich)* "together," pronounced [tsuː'glaeç], and *Zugluft (Zug + Luft)* "draft," pronounced ['tsuːkˌlʊft]. The difference is in some instances more striking in singing than in speaking. A combination such as *bl, kr, fl* will be launched on one note if it belongs to one element; if, however, the combination is composed of parts of two elements, the first part will be sung on one note, the second on the next.

A. Prefixes

Since a number of prefixes end in consonants, a variety of consonant combinations occurs in words containing prefixes. The prefix always constitutes a separate element, and its final consonant should not be tied over to the next element.

Exercise 7.8

1. Pronounce the following words.
2. Transcribe them into the IPA.
3. Indicate how the consonant cluster in each word would be divided by placing a slash between the sounds; for example, *zugleich* [tsuː/'glaeç] "together."
   1. abrennen, abbrennen, angehen, Vorrat, Verrat
   2. entrüstet, unnötig, fortrennen, herritt, Hinnahme

B. Suffixes

Since a number of suffixes begin with consonants, a variety of consonant combinations occurs in words containing suffixes. The suffix always constitutes a separate element, and a final consonant in the preceding element should not be tied over to an initial consonant in the suffix.

Exercise 7.9

1. Pronounce the following words.
2. Transcribe them into the IPA.
3. Indicate how the consonant cluster in each word would be divided by placing a slash between the sounds; for example, *lieblich* ['liːp/lɪç] "lovable."

   unglaublich

   endlich

   sorglos

   Derbheit

   verschiebbar

C. Compounds

In compounds also, problem clusters may be formed at the junction of two elements. Here too, each element is pronounced separately, and consonant sounds are not blended across the boundary. Observe the separation of consonants in the compound *Zugluft* ['tsuːk/ˌlʊft] "draft."

The final consonants of the connecting elements *(e)s, er, (e)n* will always be separated from following consonants, as in *Todestag* ['toːdəs/ˌtɑːk] "day of death."

Exercise 7.10

1. Pronounce the following words.
2. Transcribe them into the IPA.
3. Indicate how the consonant clusters in each word would be divided by placing a slash between the sounds.
   1. arglistig, Arbeitstisch, Betstunde, Dankrede
   2. Donnerstag, Festrede, huldreich, Bergland

D. Inflection

Problem consonant clusters are not generally formed by the addition of inflectional endings.

It should be clear from the foregoing section on consonant clusters that some knowledge of German is necessary in order to determine how to divide some problem clusters. The novice cannot really be expected to know how to divide *Zugluft* or *zugleich*. Or consider the unusual form *erblich*. As a verb meaning "grew pale," it is divided into the prefix *er-* and the root *blich* and is pronounced [ɛʁ/'blɪç]. As an adjective meaning "hereditary," it is divided into the root *erb-* and the suffix *-lich* and is pronounced ['ɛrp/lɪç]. It is clear from these examples that it is important to learn to recognize the prefixes, suffixes, and inflectional endings. Then, as consonant clusters are treated in greater detail in the following sections, it should be easier for the singer to develop some skill in determining how to divide them.

IV. Glottal Stop

The glottal stop, indicated in this text by the symbol [|], is the brief stoppage of air before articulating a following vowel. It can prevent *an aim* [ən |eɪm] from sounding like *a name* [ə neɪm]. In some accents, this sound is substituted for *t* in words like *bottle* ['bɑ|l].

In German, every word beginning with a vowel is preceded by a glottal stop, although most singers do not use a glottal attack on every word beginning with a vowel. This is just the reverse of French, in which glottal stops are avoided and a final consonant in one word is tied over to a following word beginning with a vowel.

Exercise 7.11

Practice separating with a glottal stop the words beginning with a vowel in the following phrases:

1. die alte Amme

2. der erste Akt

3. ein altes Erbe

Most texts and references use the symbol [ʔ] for glottal stop. We have chosen the symbol [|] because this is what appears in Siebs. There it is stressed that the symbol is used not so much to indicate a glottal stop per se as a break in the legato flow within a word. Thus the symbol [|] appears in Siebs primarily within a word rather than at the beginning. Although many singers feel that it is important to begin most words starting with a vowel with a glottal stop, we will focus our attention on its use within words, where it can serve to separate elements.

A. Prefixes

As we have pointed out, any prefix constitutes a separate element and should be pronounced as a unit. If the prefix is followed by a vowel, the vowel will usually be preceded by a glottal stop, as in *erinnern* [ɛʁ|ˈɪnɐn] "remember," *beachten* [bəˈ|axtən] "take heed."

The prefixes *her-, hin-, dar-,* and *vor-* represent a special case. When they are combined with another prefix beginning with a vowel, there is no glottal stop and the final consonant is drawn to the following syllable, as in *heran* [hɛˈran] "hither," *hinan* [hɪˈnan] "upward," *daran* [daˈran] "to it," and *voran* [foˈran] "forward." However, when *her-, hin-, dar-,* and *vor-* appear before an element other than another prefix, they are pronounced as a unit and followed by a glottal stop if the element begins with a vowel, as in *Vorahnung* [ˈfoːʁ|aːnuŋ] "premonition." As a general rule, of these four prefixes only *vor-* will appear before an element which begins with a vowel but is not a prefix.

Exercise 7.12

Pronounce the following words, using a glottal stop where appropriate:

1. abändern, beobachten, aneignen, auferstehen, fortan

2. ausatmen, einatmen, entarten, erinnern, überantwortet

3. geahnt, geehrt, vereint, Mitarbeiter, unterirdisch

4. nachahmen, überall, vorangehen, vorauseilen, Vorort

5. daraus, mißachten, herannahen, uralt, unendlich

6. beiordnen, beirren, durchirren, wegessen, umändern

7. hineingehen, zuerst, forteilen, verteilen, Vorahnung

Exercise 7.13

Transcribe the words in Exercise 7.12 into the IPA. Be sure to note glottal stop with [|].

B. Suffixes

A suffix will *not* ordinarily be separated from a preceding element by a glottal stop. For example, in *Ahnung* ['ɑːnʊŋ] "notion," the suffix *-ung* is not preceded by a glottal stop.

C. Compounds

In a compound word, an element that begins with a vowel will normally be preceded by a glottal stop, as in *bergab* [bɛɾkǀʔap] "downhill." It will require a fair amount of experience and some knowledge of German to understand how to divide some words.

Exercise 7.14

Pronounce the following words, using a glottal stop where necessary:

1. bergauf, jahrein, kläräugig, herzergreifend, Hufeisen
2. Todesahnung, liebentflammten, Blutacker, Klageruf
3. gottergeben, Götterfunken, Donnerschlag, herzerschütternd, jahraus
4. Liebeserklärung, Meisterehre, Abendessen, unterdessen, Aberglaube
5. bandartig, Blasinstrument, bösartig, Drehorgel, Dreieck
6. ehrerbietig, Handarbeit, Lesart, Tonart

D. Inflection

An inflectional ending will *not* normally be separated from a preceding element by a glottal stop; for example, in *bebest* ['beːbəst], there is no glottal stop before the ending *-est*.

Excerpts

Read the following excerpts aloud, paying careful attention to the use of glottal stop:

1. ihrem Aug eilt Amor zu
   An Silvia
   Shakespeare (Bauernfeld)/Schubert

2. Geuß nicht so laut der liebentflammten Lieder
   Tonreichen Schall
   Vom Blütenast des Apfelbaums hernieder,
   O Nachtigall!
   An die Nachtigall
   Hölty/Brahms

3. Ich saß zu deinen Füßen in Waldeseinsamkeit;
   Windesatmen, Sehnen ging durch die Wipfel breit.
   In stummem Ringen senkt' ich das Haupt in deinen Schoß,
   und meine bebenden Hände um deine Knie ich schloß.
   Die Sonne ging hinunter, der Tag verglühte all.
   Ferne, ferne, ferne sang eine Nachtigall.
   In Waldeseinsamkeit
   Lemcke/Brahms

8 The Sounds of *b, d, g*

The consonants *b, d, g,* and *s* (see Chapter 10 for *s*) are voiced when they stand before a vowel which is in the same element or before *l* or *r* in the same element. You will recall from Chapter 7 that, in general, when these consonants occur before a consonant, at the end of a word, or at the end of an element, they become unvoiced. You will also recall that when they appear before *l, n,* or *r* in inflected forms and derivatives of words ending in *-el, -en,* or *-er,* they are not usually unvoiced.

A double consonant occurring within one element usually follows the same rules for pronunciation as a single consonant, although some feel that it should be somewhat longer in duration.

SECTION 1: *b, bb*

[b]

When followed in the same element by a vowel, *l,* or *r,* the letter *b* is pronounced [b], as in *Eber* [ˈeːbəʁ] "boar," *geblickt* [ɡəˈblɪkt] "glimpsed," *verbracht* [fɛʁˈbʁaχt] "spent." Before *l, n,* or *r* in an inflected form or derivative of a word ending in *-el, -en,* or *-er,* the *b* is considered part of the same element and is pronounced [b], as in *übler* [ˈyːblɐʁ] (*übel*) "evil."

[p]

In general, when *b* appears before a consonant, at the end of a word, or at the end of an element, it is pronounced [p]: *Liebster* [ˈliːpstəʁ] "dearest," *Grab* [ɡʁɑːp] "grave," *abändern* [ˈapˌɛndəʁn] "transform," *lieblich* [ˈliːplɪç][1] "dear," *abreisen* [ˈapʁaezən] "depart."

In Chapter 7, we used the slash [/] to indicate a separation in the pronunciation of consonants, assuring that no blend occurs. In order to minimize the number of symbols to be learned, we will not use the slash in this and the following sections; however, the singer should remain aware that in words like

---

[1]Some singers prefer to voice the *b* before *-lich* and certain other suffixes: [ˈliːblɪç].

lieblich and *abreisen, bl* and *br* do not form blends and should be pronounced with their respective elements.

Exercise 8.1

Contrast voiced and unvoiced *b* in the following pairs of related words:

1.	lebe	lebt
2.	grabe	gräbst
3.	geben	gibt
4.	halber	Halbinsel
5.	leben	leblos
6.	lieben	liebäugeln

bb

One Element

In the few words in which *bb* occurs within the same element, it is pronounced according to the rules for *b,* for example, *Ebbe* [ˈɛbə] "ebb tide," *verebbt* [fɛʁˈ|ɛpt] "ebbed."

Two Elements

In most instances *bb* occurs at the junction of two elements, in which case it is pronounced [pb], as in *abbauen* [ˈapˌbɑoən] "dismantle."

Exercise 8.2

Pronounce the following words, paying careful attention to the pronunciation of *b*:

1. bitte, ob, obwohl, lobe, lobt, Lob
2. liebe, lieb, lieblich, geliebt, lieber, Liebchen, Liebschaft
3. schwebt, gibst, trübst, lebst, Leben, grubst
4. Obst, tobt, bebt, übt, Trieb, Triebe
5. Erlebnis, Trübsal, strebsam, leblos, lebhaft
6. abrennen, abbrennen, herabsehen, hinabeilen
7. vergebe, vergeblichen, geblichen, geblasen, gebt, unablässig
8. ablassen, abblassen, erblassen, gebet, Gebet, Verlöbnis
9. Himbeere, aberkennen, Aberglaube, Abende, Schreibpapier
10. grabe, Grab, Grabrede, Krabbe, Ebne, biblisch

Exercise 8.3

Transcribe the words in Exercise 8.2 into the IPA.

Tape

Read the following song text onto a tape without stopping the recorder:

Du meine Seele, du mein Herz,
Du meine Wonn', o du mein Schmerz,
Du meine Welt, in der ich lebe,
Mein Himmel, du, darein ich schwebe,
O du mein Grab, in das hinab
Ich ewig meinen Kummer gab!
Du bist die Ruh, du bist der Frieden,
Du bist vom Himmel mir beschieden,
Daß du mich liebst, macht mich mir wert,
Dein Blick hat mich vor mir verklärt,

Du hebst mich liebend über mich,
Mein guter Geist, mein bessres Ich!

Widmung
Rückert/Schumann

Song   Sing the following song, paying special attention to the pronunciation of *b*.

Ach, wie ist's möglich dann

Ach,   wie   ist's___   mög - lich   dann,___   daß   ich   dich   las - sen   kann!
Blau   ist   ein___   Blü - me - lein,___   das   heißt   Ver - giß - nicht - mein.
Wär'   ich   ein___   Vö - ge - lein,___   wollt'   ich   bald   bei   dir   sein,

Hab'   dich   von   Her - zen___   lieb,___   das   glau - be   mir!
Dies   Blüm - lein   leg'   ans___   Herz___   und   denk   an   mich!
scheut'   Falk'   und   Ha - bicht___   nicht,___   flög'   schnell   zu   dir.

Du   hast   die   See - le   mein___   so   ganz   ge - nom - men ein,
Stirbt   Blüt'   und   Hoff - nung gleich,___   wir   sind   an   Lie - be   reich;
Schöss'   mich   ein   Jä - ger   tot,___   fiel'   ich   in   dei - nen   Schoß;

daß   ich   kein'   an - dre   lieb'   als   dich   al - lein.
denn   die   stirbt   nie   bei   mir,   das   glau - be   mir!
säh'st du   mich   trau - rig   an,   gern   stürb'   ich   dann.

SECTION 2:   *d, dt, dd*

[d]

When followed in the same element by a vowel or *r*, the letter *d* is pronounced [d], as in *Ader* ['ɑːdəʁ] "artery," *bedrohen* [bəˈdroːən] "threaten."

Before *l*, *n*, or *r* in an inflected form or derivative of a word ending in *-el*, *-en*, or *-er*, the *d* is considered part of the same element and is pronounced [d], as in *edler* ['eːdləʁ] (< edel) "noble."

[t]

In general, when *d* appears before a consonant, at the end of a word, or at the end of an element, it is pronounced [t], as in *freundlich* ['frɔøntlɪç][2] "friendly," *Freund* [frɔønt] "friend," *fremdartig* ['frɛmtˌɑːrtɪç] "strange."

Exercise 8.4   Contrast voiced and unvoiced *d* in the following pairs of related words:

1. Lieder   Lied
2. Ende   Endergebnis
3. laden   lädst
4. Stunde   stündlich
5. Kinder   Kind
6. Erde   Erdball

dt

One Element   When the combination *dt* appears within one element, it is pronounced [t], as in *Städte* ['ʃtɛːtə] "cities."

---

[2]Some singers prefer to voice *d* before *-lich* and certain other suffixes: ['frɔøndlɪç].

Two Elements

If *dt* represents parts of two different elements, then it is pronounced [tt], as in *Handtuch* [ˈhantˌtuːχ] "towel."

dd

One Element

In the handful of words in which *dd* occurs within the same element, it is pronounced according to the rules for *d*, as in *Widder* [ˈvɪdəʁ] "ram."

Two Elements

Usually, *dd* represents parts of two elements and is pronounced [td], as in *Raddampfer* [ˈraːtˌdampfəʁ] "side-wheeler."

Exercise 8.5

Pronounce the following words according to the rules for pronunciation of *d*:

1. Dame, bedacht, Feder, Verdruß, endlich, lädt
2. Band, Bande, bandartig, Bandreif, Todesbanden
3. Wildnis, endlos, Feindschaft, Mädchen, widmen, widrig
4. Waldhüter, Lindrung, Geld, seidnes, Waldeinsamkeit
5. tödlich, redlich, Redner, redselig, beredsam, golden, Gold, goldne
6. südlich, sündhaft, Abenddämmerung, verheddern
7. Erde, irdisch, Erdteil, erdreisten, huldreichstes, Handarbeit
8. Abendröte, Abendstern, Abendessen, anordnen

Excerpts

Read the following excerpts aloud:

1. Was vermeid' ich denn die Wege,
   Wo die andern Wandrer gehn . . .
   Der Wegweiser (Winterreise)
   Müller/Schubert

2. Im Felde schleich' ich still und wild,
   Gespannt mein Feuerrohr,
   Da schwebt so licht dein liebes Bild,
   Dein süßes Bild mir vor.

   Du wandelst jetzt wohl still und mild
   Durch Feld und liebes Thal,
   Und ach, mein schnell verrauschend Bild,
   Stellt sich dir's nicht einmal?

   Mir ist es, denk' ich nur an dich,
   Als in den Mond zu sehn;
   Ein stiller Friede kommt auf mich,
   Weiß nicht, wie mir geschehn.
   Jägers Abendlied
   Goethe/Schubert, Reichardt

3. Ich hatt' ihn ausgeträumet,
   Der Kindheit friedlich schönen Traum,
   Ich fand allein mich, verloren
   Im öden, unendlichen Raum.

Du Ring an meinem Finger
Chamisso/Schumann

Song   Sing the following song, concentrating on the pronunciation of *d*.

Gold und Silber

Gold und Sil - ber lieb' ich sehr, könnt' es auch ge - brau - chen;
Seht, wie blinkt der gold' - ne Wein hier in mei - nem Be - cher;
Doch viel schö - ner ist das Gold, das vom Lok - ken - köpf - chen

hätt' ich nur ein gan - zes Meer, mich hin - ein - zu - tau - chen.
hört, wie klin - gen sil - ber - hell Lie - der fro - her Ze - cher.
mei - nes trau - ten Lieb - chens rollt in zwei blon - den Zöpf - chen.

's braucht ja nicht ge - prägt zu sein, hab' es sonst auch ger - ne
Daß die Zeit einst gol - den war, möcht' ich nicht be - strei - ten,
Dar - um fröh - lich, lie - bes Kind, laß uns her - zen, küs - sen,

gleich des Mon - des Sil - ber - schein und der gold' - nen Ster - ne,
denkt man doch im Sil - ber - haar gern ver - gang' - ner Zei - ten,
bis die Lok - ken sil - bern sind und wir schei - den müs - sen,

gleich des Mon - des Sil - ber - schein und der gold' - nen Ster - ne.
denkt man doch im Sil - ber - haar gern ver - gang' - ner Zei - ten.
bis die Lok - ken sil - bern sind und wir schei - den müs - sen.

SECTION 3: *g, ig, gn, gg*

[g]

When followed in the same element by a vowel, *l,* or *r,* the letter *g* is pronounced [g], as in *klagen* ['klɑːgən] "lament," *beglücken* [bə'glʏkən] "make happy," *begrüßen* [bə'gɾyːsən] "greet."

Before *l, n,* or *r* in an inflected form or derivative of a word ending in *-el, -en,* or *-er,* the *g* is considered part of the same element and is pronounced [g], as in *eigner* ['aegnɐʁ] "own."

[k]

In general, when *g* appears before a consonant, at the end of a word, or at the end of an element, it is pronounced [k], as in *klagt* [klɑːkt] "laments," *lag* [lɑːk] "lay," *kläglich* ['klɛːklɪç][3] "wretched," *bergab* [bɛɾk'ap] "downhill."

[ʒ]

In some words of French origin, *g* is pronounced [ʒ]. Memorize the following:

Genie	[ʒe'niː]	"genius"
genieren	[ʒe'niːɾən]	"embarrass"
Gendarm	[ʒan'daɾm]	"gendarm"
Orange	[o'ɾɑ̃ʒə]	"orange"
Rage	['ɾɑːʒə]	"rage"
Regie	[ɾe'ʒiː]	"direction" (theatrical)
Regisseur	[ɾeʒisøːɾ]	"director"
Courage	[ku'ɾɑːʒə]	"courage"
arrangieren	[aɾɑ̃'ʒiːɾən]	"arrange"

Exercise 8.6   Contrast voiced and unvoiced *g* in the following pairs of related words:

1. lagen   lagst
2. bewegen   bewegt
3. Zuge   Zugabteil
4. mögen   möglich
5. Zeuge   Zeugnis
6. hege   hegt

---

[3]Some singers prefer to voice *g* before *-lich* and certain other suffixes: ['klɛːglɪç].

ig

[ɪç]

At the end of a word or before a consonant, *-ig* is pronounced [ɪç], as in *heilig* ['haelɪç] "holy" and *heiligt* ['haelɪçt] "consecrates."

[ɪg]

Before a vowel, *-ig* is pronounced [ɪg], as in *heilige* ['haelɪgə] "holy."

[ɪk]

Before a syllable ending in the sound [ç] (usually the suffix *-lich*), *-ig* is pronounced [ɪk], as in *königlich* ['kø:nɪklɪç] "royal."

Exercise 8.7　　Contrast the pronunciation of *-ig* in the following pairs of related words:

1. wichtigen	wichtig
2. lockige	lockig
3. beleidigen	beleidigt
4. ewige	Ewigkeit
5. brünstige	brünstigsten
6. wenige	wenigstens

gn

One Element　　If the combination *gn* appears within one element, it is pronounced [gn], as in *Gnom* [gno:m] "gnome."

gg

One Element　　In the few words in which *gg* occurs within the same element, it is pronounced according to the rules for *g*, as in *Flagge* ['flagə] "flag." The double consonant requires more breath support than the single consonant.

Two Elements　　In most instances, *gg* represents parts of two elements and is pronounced [kg], as in *weggehen* ['vɛkˌge:ən] "go away."

Exercise 8.8　　Pronounce the following words, using the rules for the pronunciation of *g:*

1. lege, legst, gelegt, Belegs, legte, begleiten
2. Berg, Bergland, Berggeist, Roggen, weggetan
3. Flug, Flugs, Fluggast, flügge, zugleich, Zugluft
4. innig, innige, inniglich, Genie, General, möglich
5. eigen, geeignet, begegnen, behaglich, wenigstens

6. arg, arglos, regnet, Zögling, zogst, Betrugs

7. vergnügt, Traurigkeit, segnen, brünstigsten, Bergnymphe

8. holdseliglich, kreuzigte, Heiligtum, Königreich, bergauf

9. arglistig, jeglich, geglichen, gehegt, Gnade, Gegner

l0. vergnügen, wonniglich, fügte, bewogst, heilges, sorglos

Exercise 8.9   Transcribe the words in Exercise 8.8 into the IPA.

Excerpts   Read the following excerpts aloud:

1. Es grünet ein Nußbaum vor dem Haus,
   Duftig,
   Luftig
   Breitet er blättrig die Äste aus.
   > *Der Nußbaum*
   > *Mosen/Schumann*

2. Der Mond scheint hell, der Rasen grün
   Ist gut zu unserm Begegnen,
   Du trägst ein Schwert und nickst so kühn,
   Dein' Liebschaft will ich segnen!

   Und als erschien der lichte Tag,
   Was fand er auf der Heide!
   Ein Toter in den Blumen lag
   Zu einer Falschen Leide.
   > *Verrat*
   > *Lemcke/Brahms*

3. Als ich befriedigt,
   Freudigen Herzens,
   Sonst dem Geliebten im Arme lag,
   Immer noch rief er,
   Sehnsucht im Herzen,
   Ungeduldig den heutigen Tag.
   Helft mir, ihr Schwestern,
   Helft mir verscheuchen
   Eine thörichte Bangigkeit;
   Daß ich mit klarem
   Aug' ihn empfange,
   Ihn, die Quelle der Freudigkeit.
   > *Helft mir, ihr Schwestern (Frauenliebe und -leben)*
   > *Chamisso/Schumann*

4 Durchzuckt von seligsten Genusses Schmerz,
   des heiligsten Blutes Quell
   fühl' ich sich gießen in mein Herz:
   des eignen sündigen Blutes Gewell'.
   > *Parsifal, Act I*
   > *Wagner*

Song   Sing the following song, paying special attention to the pronunciation of *g*.

Ich hatt' einen Kameraden

Ich hatt' ei - nen Ka - me - ra - den, ei - nen bes - ser'n find'st du
Eine Ku - gel kam ge - flo - gen, gilt sie mir oder gilt sie
Will mir die Hand noch rei - chen, der - weil ich e - ben

nit. Die ___ Trom - mel schlug zum Strei - te, er ___
dir? Ihn ___ hat es weg - ge - ris - sen, er ___
lad': "Kann ___ dir die Hand nicht ge - ben, bleib ___

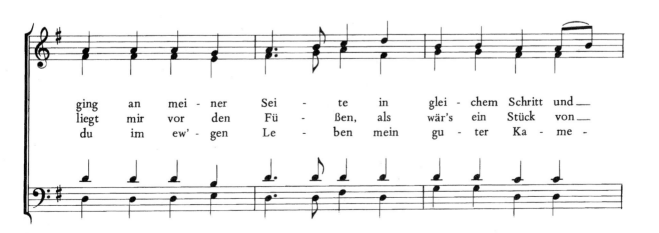

ging an mei - ner Sei - te in glei - chem Schritt und ___
liegt mir vor den Fü - ßen, als wär's ein Stück von ___
du im ew'gen Le - ben mein gu - ter Ka - me -

Tritt,   in   glei - chem Schritt   und ___ Tritt.
mir,   als   wär's   ein Stück   von ___ mir.
rad,   mein   gu - ter   Ka   -   me -   rad.

9 Monophthongs: Part II

I n Chapter 6, general rules were stated regarding the length and quality of the vowels of that chapter: *i, ü(y), e, ö, o, u.* The vowels *a, ä* and *ie* were not included in Chapter 6 because they deviate from these rules somewhat.

SECTION 1: *a*

Although many singers and voice teachers feel that no *qualitative* distinction should be made between long and short *a*, most speakers do make a distinction, and many references reflect the distinction in their transcriptions. Siebs does not reflect the qualitative distinction.

[ɑː]

Long [ɑː] (sometimes referred to as "dark" *a*) is more of a back vowel and is pronounced about like *a* in English *father*.[1] Like other long vowels, *a* is regularly pronounced long: (1) before *h*, as in *ahnen* ['ɑːnən] "to sense"; (2) doubled, as in *Saal* [zɑːl] "hall"; and (3) before a single consonant, as in *Amen* ['ɑːmɛn].

Exceptions

In some words *a* is long before two or more consonants.[2] Memorize the following:

[1]In speaking, at least, the vowel *a* is *open* when long and *closed* when short.
[2]Normally, *a* is short before *ß, ch,* and *r* + consonant, as expected.

1. before *ß* [3] in:

Spaß	"fun"
saß	"sat"
Straße	"street"

(note that *a* is short, as expected, in *daß*)

2. before *ch* in:

nach	"after, toward"

(however, the *a* in this element is short in *Nachbar* [ˈnaχbɑːɾ] "neighbor")

brach	"broke"
stach	"pricked"
Schmach	"disgrace"
Sprache	"language, speech"

3. before *r* + consonant in:

Art	"kind, sort"
Bart	"beard"
zart	"gentle"
Arzt	"doctor"

4. in some other words:

Bratsche	"viola"
atmen	"breathe"
Magd	"maid"
Jagd	"hunt"

Exercise 9.1   Pronounce:

1. Staat, fragen, Mahl, Banane, Trübsal
2. Kahn, Grab, prahlen, fragt, labt

[a]

Short [a] (sometimes referred to as "bright" *a*) is more of a front vowel and is similar to the first element in the English diphthong [aɪ], as in *ice* [aɪs].[4] The pronunciation of *a* is regularly short before two or more consonants, as in *Macht* [maχt] "power."

[3]See note on *ß*, p. 35.
[4]See note 1.

Exceptions

In a number of words, *a* is pronounced short before a single consonant. Memorize the following:

1. short words:

an	"to, at"

(and its many compounds, such as *heran, hinan*)

am	"to the, at the"
ab	"away"

(and its many compounds, such as *herab, hinab*)

man	"one, someone"
das	"that, the"
was	"what"
hat	"has"

2. other words:

Monat	"month"
Heimat	"home"
Bräutigam	"groom"

Exercise 9.2

Contrast [ɑː] and [a] in the following pairs:

1. Maße   Masse
2. Saat   satt
3. Staat   Stadt
4. Schlaf   schlaff
5. Haken   Hacken
6. kam   Kamm
7. Kahn   kann
8. rast   Rast
9. nagt   nackt

The English-speaking singer should be especially careful about the pronunciation of *a* in unstressed syllables. Although the pronunciation of unstressed *a* is reduced to [ə] in English, as in *America* [əˈmɛrɪkə], in German the pronunciation is clearly an *a*-sound, as in *Amerika* [ɑˈmeːrikɑ], Schumann [ˈʃuːman]. The unstressed prefix *da-*, as in *dafür* [dɑˈfyːʁ],[5] tends to be particularly troublesome for English-speaking people.

---

[5]Although the quality of [ɑ] is maintained, length is not indicated because it is in an unstressed syllable.

Exercise 9.3   Pronounce:

     1. Monat, Tag, Gasse, wandern, schwarz

     2. fragen, sagt, Abend, barfuß, wach

     3. Bach, ach, machen, Schmach, brach

     4. Blatt, Hand, Nachtigall, Wahn, sahen

     5. Karte, Pappeln, naß, saß, Wasser

     6. fahle, falle, sanft, alles, fragt

     7. Schumann, Telemann, Richard

Exercise 9.4   Transcribe the words in Exercise 9.3 into the IPA.

Excerpts   1. Nun hast du mir den ersten Schmerz getan,
      Der aber traf.
      Du schläfst, du harter, unbarmherz'ger Mann,
      Den Todesschlaf.
         Frauenliebe und -leben
         Chamisso/Schumann

     2. Um Mitternacht
      hab' ich gedacht
      hinaus in dunkle Schranken.
      Es hat kein Lichtgedanken
      mir Trost gebracht
      um Mitternacht.
         Um Mitternacht
         Rückert/Mahler

     3. Ich unglücksel'ger Atlas! eine Welt,
      Die ganze Welt der Schmerzen, muß ich tragen.
      Ich trage Unerträgliches, und brechen
      Will mir das Herz im Leibe.
         Der Atlas
         Heine/Schubert

     4. Allein und abgetrennt von aller Freude,
      seh' ich ans Firmament nach jener Seite.
         Lied der Mignon
         Goethe/Schubert

Song   Sing the following song, concentrating on the pronunciation of *a*.

Wanderschaft

Das   Wan - dern ist des   Mül - lers Lust, das   Wan - dern ist des
Vom   Was - ser ha - ben   wir's ge - lernt, vom   Was - ser ha - ben
Das   seh'n wir auch den   Rä - dern ab, das   seh'n wir auch den
O   Wan - dern, Wan - dern   mei - ne Lust, o   Wan - dern, Wan - dern

Mül - lers Lust, das   Wan - dern!   Das muß ein   schlech - ter __
wir's ge - lernt, vom   Was - ser!   Das hat nicht Ruh' __ bei __
Rä - dern ab, den   Rä - dern!   Die gar nicht ger - ne __
mei - ne Lust, o   Wan - dern!   Herr Mei - ster und __ Frau

Mül - ler sein, dem   nie - mals fiel __ das __   Wan - dern ein, dem
Tag und Nacht, ist   stets auf   Wan - der - schaft be - dacht, ist
stil - le steh'n und   sich bei   Tag __ nicht __ mü - de dreh'n, und
Mei - ste - rin, laßt   mich in   Frie - den __ wei - ter - zieh'n, laßt

nie - mals fiel das Wan - dern ein, das Wan   -   dern.
stets auf Wan - der - schaft be - dacht, das Was   -   ser!
sich bei Tag nicht mü - de dreh'n, die Rä   -   der!
mich in Frie - den wei - ter - zieh'n und Wan   -   dern.

Tape   Read the text of the above song onto a tape, without stopping the tape.

SECTION 2:   *ä*

[ɛː]

In singing, *ä* is pronounced as an open vowel even if it is long: [ɛː].[6] It is generally pronounced long before *h,* as in *Mähne* [ˈmɛːnə] "mane," and before a
single consonant, as in *spät* [ʃpɛːt] "late."

Exceptions

In some words, *ä* is long before two or more consonants. Memorize the
following:

Gemälde	"painting"
Rätsel	"riddle"
Städte	"cities"
zärtlich	"gentle"
Gespräch	"conversation"

[ɛ]

The pronunciation of *ä* is regularly short before two or more consonants, as
in *Händel* [ˈhɛndəl].

Exercise 9.5   Contrast long and short *ä* in the following pairs:

1. stähle   Ställe
2. lähme   Lämmer

---

[6]In speaking, long *ä* is frequently pronounced closed: [eː]; but this pronunciation is to be avoided in
singing.

3. Städte   Stätte

4. läst   läßt

Exercise 9.6   Pronounce the following words containing *ä*:

1. Händel, Götterdämmerung, Ländler, Bäcker

2. Jäger, Hähne, Mädchen, krähen, erklärt

3. dämpfen, ändern, ängstlich, Ärger, fährt

4. Bäche, lästern, Verräter, Blätter, Nächte

5. jähes, Ähre, Träne, Märchen, grämlich

Excerpts   Read the following excerpts aloud:

1. Väter, laßt euch's Warnung sein,
   sperrt die Zuckerplätzchen ein!
   sperrt die jungen Mädchen ein!
   Warnung
   Unknown/Mozart

2. Du Doppelgänger, du bleicher Geselle!
   Was äffst du nach mein Liebesleid,
   Das mich gequält auf dieser Stelle
   So manche Nacht, in alter Zeit?
   Der Doppelgänger
   Heine/Schubert

3. Ängste, quäle
   Dich nicht länger, meine Seele!
   Freu dich! schon sind da und dorten
   Morgenglocken wach geworden.
   In der Frühe
   Mörike/Wolf

Song   Sing the following song, paying close attention to the pronunciation of *ä*.

Die Gedanken sind frei

ra - ten? Sie flie - hen vor - bei wie __ nächt - li - che
glük - ket, doch al - les in der Still' und __ wie es sich
al - len, sie tut mir al - lein am __ be - sten ge -
sa - gen und will mich auch __ nim - mer mit __ Gril - len mehr

Schat - ten. Kein Mensch kann sie wis - sen, kein Jä - ger er -
schik - ket. Mein Wunsch, mein Be - geh - ren kann nie - mand mir
fal - len. Ich sitz' nicht al - lei - ne bei mei - nem Glas
pla - gen. Man kann ja im Her - zen stets la - chen und

schie - ßen, es blei - bet da - bei: die Ge - dan - ken sind frei.
weh - ren, es blei - bet da - bei: die Ge - dan - ken sind frei.
Wei - ne, mein Mäd - chen da - bei: die Ge - dan - ken sind frei.
scher - zen und den - ken da - bei: die Ge - dan - ken sind frei.

SECTION 3: *ie*

[iː]

Except under the conditions outlined below, *ie* is pronounced [iː], as in *die* [diː] "the," *fliegen* [ˈfliːgən] "fly." Thus it is long and closed even before more than one consonant, as in *Biest* [biːst] "beast."

A. Final *-ie*

1. [iː]
   In some words of foreign origin (usually Greek), final *-ie* is stressed and pronounced [iː], as in *Melodie* [melo'diː]. Many of these words are scientific, such as *Geographie, Philosophie.* However, the singer should become familiar with the following examples:

Elegie	Partie
Galerie	Phantasie
Genie	Poesie
Melancholie	Symphonie
Melodie	

2. [jə]
   In other words of foreign origin (usually Latin), final *-ie* is unstressed and pronounced [jə], as in *Familie* [fɑmiːljə]. The singer should learn to recognize the following words of this type:

Akazie	Historie
Arie	Hortensie
Bestie	Hostie
Dahlie	Kamelie
Familie	Kastanie
Fuchsie	Komödie
Gardenie	Lilie
Glorie	Linie
Grazie	Pinie
Tragödie	

B. Final *-ien*

1. [iːən]
   In the plurals of words of the type *Melodie,* final *-ien* is pronounced [iːən], and the stress is on the next to last syllable: *Melodien* [melo'diːən].

2. [jən]
   In the plurals of words of the type *Familie* the stress falls on the same syllable as in the singular, and final *-ien* is pronounced [jən]: *Familien* [fɑ'miːljən]. Also in geographical names, *-ien* is pronounced [jen], for example, *Belgien* ['bɛlgjən]. The following examples might occur in vocal literature:

   Asien

   Belgien

   Indien

Italien

Spanien

Exercise 9.7   Pronounce the following words:

1. Lied, fließen, riechen, Ziel, studieren

2. Kastanien, Melodien, verdient, Lilien, fliehen

3. Spanien, Symphonie, probieren, Begierde, Brief

4. Partie, Glorie, Riemen, wieder, Priester

5. liegen, Pinien, liebt, hielt, hier, schrie

Excerpts   Read the following excerpts aloud:

1. Die Rose, die Lilie, die Taube, die Sonne,
   Die liebt' ich einst alle in Liebeswonne.

   Die Rose, die Lilie
   Heine/Schumann

2. Erzeugt von heißer Phantasie,
   In einer schwärmerischen Stunde zur Welt gebrachte,
   Geht zu Grunde, ihr Kinder der Melancholie!

   Als Luise die Briefe
   Baumberg/Mozart

Tape   Read the following song text onto a tape without stopping the recorder:

Rosen brach ich nachts mir am dunklen Hage;
Süßer hauchten Duft sie als je am Tage;
Doch verstreuten reich die bewegten Äste
Tau, der mich näßte.

Auch der Küsse Duft mich wie nie berückte,
Die ich nachts vom Strauch deiner Lippen pflückte;
Doch auch dir, bewegt im Gemüt gleich jenen,
Tauten die Tränen!

Sapphische Ode
Schmidt/Brahms

10 The Sounds of *s* and Its Combinations

SECTION 1:   *s, ß, ss*

[z]

B efore a vowel, *s* is pronounced [z], as in *singen* ['zɪŋən] "sing," *einsam* ['aenzɑːm] "lonely." When *s* occurs before *l, n,* or *r* in an inflected form or derivative of a word ending in *-el, -en,* or *-er,* it is pronounced [z], as in *unsre* ['ʊnzɾə] (*<unser*) "our."

Exceptions

In a few words, *s* is voiceless after a voiceless (or unvoiced) consonant, even though it precedes a vowel. Learn to recognize the following:

Erbse ['ɛɾpsə]	"pea"
Krebse ['kɾeːpsə]	"crabs"
Rätsel ['ɾɛːtsəl]	"riddle"

[s]

When *s* appears before a consonant,[1] at the end of a word, or at the end of an element, it is pronounced [s], as in *Dresden* ['dɾeːsdən], *Betrugs* [bə'tɾuːks] "deceit," *Lesart* ['leːs|ɑːɾt] "version," *Grashalm* ['gɾɑːsˌhalm][2] "blade of grass."

---

[1]See "Section 2" for *sp* and *st*.

[2]Note that in German *s* and *h* do not form a combination as in English. When they appear together, they always represent parts of two different elements and are thus pronounced as [s] + [h].

Exercise 10.1   Contrast voiced and unvoiced *s* in the following pairs of related words:

1. kreisen   Kreis
2. Halse   Hals
3. Speise   speist
4. Hause   Haus
5. lösen   löst
6. lesen   lesbar

Exercise 10.2   Pronounce the following words, observing the rules for pronunciation of *s*:

1. Sage, Wiese, böse, Schicksal, seltsam
2. dies, diesen, Jesus, als, Felsen, kraus
3. gesät, Glas, Abendsonne, löst, Amsel, Friedenshaus
4. Hungersnot, Feinslieb, Königs, Guts, Rose, Linse
5. Ratsherrn, Frühlingsabendrot, heisre, holdselig
6. gesund, ringsum, losgebe, Mannsbild, Asyl
7. auserkorn, Himmelslust, boshaft, Hausarzt, Röslein
8. Todesangst, Gotteserde, gottselig, Insel, Rätsel, emsige

ß

The German character *ß* is always pronounced [s]. The character is traditionally called *Eszett*—the names of the letters *s* and *z* combined.[3] It grew out of a fusion of those two letters. In older scores, *ß* may appear as *sz;* the pronunciation will remain [s], as in *auszen* ['aosən] (provided of course that *s* and *z* do not belong to two different elements, as in *Auszug* ['aosˌtsuːk]).

The singer will find that some scores, especially those printed in the United States, do not use the character *ß,* substituting instead *ss*. However when the character *ß* is used, the following rules are rigidly observed by the printer:[4]

The character *ß* is always used:

1. at the end of a word or element, as in *muß* [mʊs] "must," *Gruß* [gruːs] "greeting," *Gußeisen* ['gʊsˌaezən] "cast iron";

2. before a consonant, as in *müßte* ['mʏstə] "would have to," *grüßte* ['gryːstə] "greeted";

3. intervocalically after a *long* vowel, as in *grüßen* ['gryːsən] "to greet."

If the character *ß* is used in a score, it follows from the above rules that the only place *ss* may appear is intervocalically after a short vowel. Thus we see that *between vowels* (and *only* between vowels) *ß* will indicate that the

---

[3] The character *ß* is also called *scharfes s* ("sharp s ").

[4] As the second edition of this book goes to press, a decision has been reached by education authorities in German-speaking countries to change the rules for the use of the symbol *ß*. We will spare the student the details of these changes. The main point for singers is that both *ß* and *ss* will still be pronounced [s].

preceding vowel is long, as in *grüßen* ['gɾyːsən], and *ss* will indicate that the preceding vowel is short, as in *müssen* ['mʏsən].

Otherwise, that is in positions 1 and 2 above, the *ß* reveals *nothing* about the length of the preceding vowel since *ß* (not *ss*) is always written finally or before a consonant.

In this book, the character *ß* is treated as a double consonant, meaning that words containing a long vowel before *ß* should be learned as exceptions. Although in fact the use of *ß* is intended in part to facilitate recognition of long vowels, the fact that it is not always used in scores makes it advisable for the singer to learn the important words containing long vowels before *ß* (see Chapters 6 and 9).

ss

One Element If *ss* appears in one element, it is pronounced [s], as in *müssen* ['mʏsən] "must."

Two Elements If an element ending in *s* is followed by an element beginning with *s,* the first *s* is not voiced. The second *s* is pronounced according to the conditions in the second element: *Aussage* ['ɑosˌzɑːgə], *aussteigen* ['ɑosˌʃtaegən]. (See also Sections 2 and 3 below.)

Exercise 10.3 Contrast *s* and *ss* (or *ß*) in the following pairs:

1. Fliesen	fließen
2. Weise	weiße
3. Nase	nasse
4. Rose	Rosse

Exercise 10.4 Pronounce the following pairs or words, noting the contrast in the vowels preceding *ß* and *ss*:

1. Maße	Masse
2. hießen	hissen
3. Schloßen	schlossen
4. Flöße	flösse
5. Buße	Busse
6. rußen	Russen

Exercise 10.5 Pronounce the following words, observing the rules for pronunciation of *ß* and *ss*:

1. Wasser, essen, vermissen, draußen, heißen
2. müssen, muß, mußte, müßte, fließen
3. grüßen, Gruß, grüßte, süß, süße, Füße, Flüsse
4. Geheimnisse, Waldessaume, dasselbe, besessen
5. Aussätzigen, fesselte, weissagen, mißachten
6. lossagen, Drossel, Liebessehnsucht, Mißverständnis

Excerpts   Read the following excerpts aloud:

1. Allnächtlich im Traume seh' ich dich,
   Und sehe dich freundlich grüßen,
   Und laut aufweinend stürz' ich mich
   Zu deinen süßen Füßen.
   > *Allnächtlich im Traume*
   > *Heine/Schumann*

2. Ich saß zu deinen Füßen in Waldeseinsamkeit;
   Windesatmen, Sehnen ging durch die Wipfel breit.
   In stummem Ringen senkt' ich das Haupt in deinen Schoß,
   Und meine bebenden Hände um deine Knie ich schloß.
   Die Sonne ging hinunter, der Tag verglühte all,
   Ferne, ferne, ferne sang eine Nachtigall.
   > *In Waldeseinsamkeit*
   > *Lemcke/Brahms*

Song   Sing the following song, paying close attention to the pronunciation of *s*.

Wir sind jung

Wir sind jung, die Welt ist of - fen, o du schö - ne, wei - te
Liegt dort hin - ter je - nem Wal - de nicht ein fer - nes, frem - des
Auf denn, auf! die Son - ne zei - ge uns den Weg durch Wald und

Welt! Uns - re Sehn - sucht, un - ser Hof - fen zieht hin -
Land? Blüht auf grü - ner Ber - ges - hal - de nicht das
Hain; geht der Tag dar - ob zur Nei - ge, leuch - te

aus   in Wald und   Feld.   Bru - der,   laß   den Kopf nicht
Blüm - lein un - be - kannt?   Laßt uns   schrei - ten im Ge -
uns   der Ster - ne   Schein.   Bru - der,   schnell den Ruck - sack

hän - gen,   kannst ja   nicht die Ster - ne   seh'n! Auf - wärts
län - de,   ü - ber Tä - ler ü - ber Höh'n! Wo sich
ü - ber,   heu - te soll's ins Wei - te   geh'n. Re - gen?

blik - ken, vor - wärts drän - gen!   Wir sind jung und das ist schön!
auch der Weg hin - wen - de: Wir sind jung und das ist schön!
Wind? wir la - chen drü - ber: Wir sind jung und das ist schön!

SECTION 2:   *st, sp*

One Element

1. [ʃt], [ʃp]

When *st* and *sp* appear at the beginning of a word or element, they are pronounced [ʃt], [ʃp], as in *stellen* ['ʃtɛlən] "place," *versprechen* [fɛʁ'ʃpɾɛçən] "promise."

Exercise 10.6   Pronounce the following words:

1. stellen, Stück, aufstellen, verstehen, Gestalt
2. spinnen, Sprache, aufspalten, versprechen, Gespenst

Exceptions

1. The superlative suffix -*st* is pronounced [st], even though it appears at the beginning of an element, regardless of what ending follows: *schnellste* ['ʃnɛlstə], *schnellstes* ['ʃnɛlstəs] "fastest."
2. The second person verb ending -*st* is always pronounced [st]: *sagst, gehst* [zɑːkst, geːst].

2. [st], [sp]

In all other cases, *st* and *sp* are pronounced [st], [sp]. Specifically, they are [st] and [sp] when they appear in one element in any position other than at the beginning, as in *beste* ['bɛstə] "best," *ist* [ɪst] "is."

Two Elements

If *st* and *sp* occur at the junction of two elements, then they are of course pronounced [s/t], [s/p], as in *austragen* ['ɑos/ˌtɾɑːgən] "carry out," *ausprägen* ['ɑos/ˌpɾɛːgən] "stamp."

Exercise 10.7   Pronounce the following words:

1. Liste, Westen, austeilen, wärmste, wärmsten
2. Wespe, Espe, auspacken, Liebespaar

Exercise 10.8   Contrast [ʃt] and [st] in words of similar appearance:

1. Gestirn	gestern
2. bestehen	besten
3. erstehen	ersten

Exercise 10.9   Pronounce the words below, following the rules for pronunciation of *st* and *sp*:

1. stehen, spät, entstehen, besprechen, zustoßen
2. lispeln, rasten, finster, Meister, schnellste
3. Strand, löste, schlugst, zuerst, Saitenspiel
4. hinsterbend, bestrebt, bester, hineinstehlen, Ostern
5. erspähen, feste, Festung, sturmestot, wegstehlen
6. liebestrunkene, Waldstrom, sternebesäeten, betrügst
7. strömt, speist, Liebeston, fernste, Wanderstab, Trost
8. unheiligster, Wehmutsstrahlen, Dienstag, Diebstahl, Fenster
9. Todestag, durchspielen, seligsten, Edelstein, erstreiten
10. Versuchungsplagen, einstürzen, Waldespracht, Hammerstreich
11. huldreichstes, Liebestraum, Festrede, Garnstricker, Gaststätte
12. Gesangstunde, Gestade, gestern, Geste, gestehen, Gerstenstange
13. garstig, Gottestisch, Götterspeise, Grabstein, Fistelstimme
14. heraustritt, Himmelstrank, Singestuhl, Singstunde, desto
15. Abendstern, Muster, Austausch, austreiben, Beständigkeit
16. Baumstamm, Beispiel, Bernstein, Betstunde, schönster, düster
17. Ruhestätte, Todesstoß, Künstler, Todespein, Siegespreis

Excerpts   1. Und zu dem Strand, dem weiten, wogenblauen,
　　Werden wir still und langsam niedersteigen.
　　　　Morgen
　　　　Mackay/Strauß

2. In deine Decke grab' ich
　　Mit einem spitzen Stein
　　Den Namen meiner Liebsten
　　Und Stund' und Tag hinein.
　　　　Auf dem Flusse
　　　　Müller/Schubert

3. Wie anders hast du mich empfangen,
　　Du Stadt der Unbeständigkeit!
　　In deinen blanken Fenstern sangen
　　Die Lerch' und Nachtigall im Streit.
　　　　Rückblick
　　　　Müller/Schubert

4. Sahst du sie gestern Abend nicht am Tore stehn,
　　Mit langem Halse nach der großen Straße sehn?
　　Wenn von dem Fang der Jäger lustig zieht nach Haus,
　　Da steckt kein sittsam Kind den Kopf zum Fenster 'naus.
　　　　Eifersucht und Stolz
　　　　Müller/Schubert

> 5. Zwar ist solche Herzensstube
>   Wohl kein schöner Fürstensaal,
>   Sondern eine finstre Grube;
>   Doch, sobald dein Gnadenstrahl
>   In dieselbe nur wird blinken,
>   Wird sie voller Sonnen dünken.
>
>   *Weihnachtsoratorium*
>   *Bach*

SECTION 3:   *sch*

One Element: [ʃ]   When *sch* appears in one element, it is pronounced [ʃ], as in *Schule* [ˈʃuːlə] "school," *schräg* [ʃrɛːk] "crooked," *rasch* [raʃ] "quickly."

Two Elements   When *s* and *ch* appear together as parts of two different elements, they will of course be pronounced separately. In this situation, *s* appears at the end of one element and is unvoiced: [s]. Usually, the following element will be the diminutive suffix *-chen,* and *ch* will be pronounced [ç], as in *Röschen* [ˈrøːsçən] "little rose."

Exercise 10.10   Pronounce the following words, following the rules for pronunciation of *sch*:

1. Schiff, schmal, schlugst, Kirsche, Kirche
2. löschen, frischem, Häschen, herrschen, Dornröschen
3. Herrschaft, Austausch, ausschwärmen, Glasscherbe
4. Bläschen, Lieschen, Geschichte, Gotteshaus, Esche
5. dreschen, verschmelzen, Grashalm, boshaft, durchschleichen

Exercise 10.11   Read the following transcription aloud:

[aχ, ɪç fyːls, ɛs ɪst fɛrˈʃvʊndən,
ˈeːvɪç hɪn deːr ˈliːbə glʏk.
ˈnɪmər kɔmt ɪːr ˈvonəʃtʊndən
ˈmaenem ˈhɛrtsən meːr tsuːˈrʏk.
ziː, taˈmiːnoː, ˈdiːzə ˈtrɛːnən ˈfliːsən,
ˈtraotər, diːr ʃaˈlaen.
fyːlst duː nɪçt deːr ˈliːbə ˈzeːnən,
zoː vɪrt ruː ɪm ˈtoːdə zaen.]

Excerpts   Read the following excerpts aloud, paying special attention to the sounds of *s* and its combinations:

1. O liebliche Wangen,
   Ihr macht mir Verlangen,
   Dies Rote, dies Weiße
   Zu schauen mit Fleiße.
   Und dies nur alleine

Ist's nicht, was ich meine;
Zu schauen, zu grüßen,
Zu rühren, zu küssen!
Ihr macht mir Verlangen,
O liebliche Wangen!
O Sonne der Wonne!
O Wonne der Sonne!
O Augen, so saugen
Das Licht meiner Augen.
O englische Sinnen!
O himmlisch Beginnen!
O Himmel auf Erden!
Magst du mir nicht werden,
O Wonne der Sonne,
O Sonne der Wonne!
O Schönste der Schönen!
Benimm mir dies Sehnen,
Komm, eile, komm, komme,
Du Süße, du Fromme!
Ach Schwester, ich sterbe,
Ich sterb', ich verderbe,
Komm, komme, komm eile,
Komm, komme, komm eile,
Benimm mir dies Sehnen,
O Schönste der Schönen.

O liebliche Wangen
Fleming/Brahms

2. O du, für den ich alles trug,
Könnt' ich zur Stelle dringen,
Wo Bosheit dich in Fesseln schlug,
Und süßen Trost dir bringen!

Fidelio
Beethoven

Tape Read the following song text onto a tape without stopping the recorder:

Meine Liebe ist grün wie der Fliederbusch,
Und mein Lieb ist schön wie die Sonne;
Die glänzt wohl herab auf den Fliederbusch
Und füllt ihn mit Duft und mit Wonne.

Meine Seele hat Schwingen der Nachtigall
Und wiegt sich in blühendem Flieder,
Und jauchzet und singet vom Duft berauscht
Viel liebestrunkene Lieder.

Meine Liebe ist Grün
Schumann/Brahms

Song Sing the following song, paying special attention to the pronunciation of *s* and its combinations.

Wem Gott will rechte Gunst

Wem Gott will rech - te Gunst er - wei - sen, den
Die Bäch - lein von den Ber - gen sprin - gen, die
Den lie - ben Gott lass' ich nur wal - ten, der

schickt er in die wei - te Welt, dem will er sei - ne Wun - der
Ler - chen schwir - ren hoch vor Lust. Wie sollt' ich nicht mit ih - nen
Bäch - lein, Ler - chen, Wald und Feld und Erd' und Him - mel will er -

wei - sen in Berg und Tal und Strom und Feld.
sin - gen aus vol - ler Kehl' und fri - scher Brust.
hal - ten, hat auch mein' Sach' aufs best' be - stellt.

CHAPTER

11 **Diphthongs**

SECTION 1:   *au*

[ɑo]

The German diphthong [ɑo], as in *Haus* [hɑos], is often equated with the English diphthong [au], as in *house* [haus]. As the symbols indicate, there is a distinct difference in pronunciation. The English diphthong begins with the front vowel [a] and ends with an open [u], whereas the German diphthong begins with the back vowel [ɑ][1] and ends with a closed [o].

Exercise 11.1   Pronounce the following words:

1. Maus, Laus, Faust, lauschen, hinauslaufen
2. rauschen, Pause, Schmaus, austauschen, auflegen

Excerpt   Es rauschen die Wipfel und schauern,
Als machten zu dieser Stund'
Um die halbversunkenen Mauern
Die alten Götter die Rund'
Schöne Fremde
Eichendorff/Schumann

SECTION 2:   *ei*

[ae]

The sound of German *ei*,[2] as in *mein* [maen][1] "my," is similar to the English diphthong [aɪ] in *mine* [maɪn] but is more closed, more clipped—hence the closed vowel [e] rather than the open vowel [ɪ] in its transcription. Note,

---

[1]Just as there is disagreement regarding the use of [a] and [ɑ] in the articulation of *a* (see Chapter 9), there are differing opinions about the initial vowel in *au* and *ei*. Siebs uses [ɑo] and [ae].

[2]Alternate, and usually older, spellings of this diphthong include *ai, ey, ay*, as in *Mai, Meyer, Bayern*.

however, that many singers tend to open the second vowel somewhat, more in the direction of [ɛ].

The singer should be exceptionally careful not to confuse *ei* with *ie*. The two are never pronounced the same. Even if they occur in different forms of the same verb, *ei* is pronounced [ae] and *ie* is pronounced [iː]: *schreibt* [ʃraept] "writes," *schriebt* [ʃriːpt] "wrote."

Exercise 11.2   Pronounce the following words:

1. Eiche, beichten, Geige, aussteigen, Kaiser

2. Heide, Waise, Weise, Wiese, Hain, Bayreuth

3. gleich, Maid, Freiheit, Saite, Seite

4. schreien, schrieen, gedeihen, gediehen, feiern

5. Melodie, Melodien, Melodei, Melodeien

Excerpts   1. Und ich geh' mit einer, die mich lieb hat,
   ruhigen Gemütes in die Kühle
   dieses weißen Hauses, in den Frieden,
   der voll Schönheit wartet, daß wir kommen.
        Freundliche Vision
        Bierbaum/Strauß

2. Heiß mich nicht reden, heiß' mich schweigen,
   Denn mein Geheimnis ist mir Pflicht;
   Ich möchte dir mein ganzes Innre zeigen,
   Allein das Schicksal will es nicht.
        Mignon II
        Goethe/Wolf

Tape   Read the following song text onto a tape without stopping the recorder:

Die Rose, die Lilie, die Taube, die Sonne,
Die liebt' ich einst alle in Liebeswonne.
Ich lieb' sie nicht mehr, ich liebe alleine
Die Kleine, die Feine, die Reine, die Eine;
Sie selber, aller Liebe Wonne,
Ist Rose und Lilie und Taube und Sonne.
        Helft mir, ihr Schwestern
        Heine/Schumann

Song   Sing the following song, paying close attention to the pronunciation of *ei*.

Ihr kleinen Vögelein

Ihr klei - nen__ Vö - ge - lein, ihr Wald - er - göt - zer - lein, ihr sü - ßen
Spitzt eu - re__ Schnä - be - lein, zwingt eu - re Stim - me - lein und fangt als__
Er ziert euch Feld und Wald so schön und man - nig - falt. Er kleid't euch
Drum stim - met__ mit mir ein, ihr sü - ßen Schrei - er - lein ihr klei - nen

Sän - ger - lein, stimmt al - le mit mir__ ein! Ich
groß und__ klein, aufs lieb - lich - ste zu__ schrein. Ich
jung und__ alt, mit Fe - dern wohl ge - stalt. Er
Pfei - fer - lein, ihr Wun - der - sän - ger - lein: Gott

will den Her - ren prei - sen mit mei - nen Lie - bes - wei - sen. Ich will von
will durch eu - er Sin - gen mich zu dem Schöp - fer schwin - gen. Ich will durch
schafft euch küh - le Sit - ze für Un - fall und für Hit - ze. Er gibt euch
Lob ist mein Er - schal - len, Gott Lob sei eu'r Er - hal - len. Gott Lob ist

Her - zens-grund ihm auf - tun mei - nen Mund!
eu - ern Ton hin - an zu Got - tes Sohn.
Speis und Trank und Mut zum Lust - ge - sang.
mein Ge - sang, Gott Lob sei eu - er Klang.

SECTION 3:   *eu, äu*

Just as the diphthongs *ei* and *au* are pronounced differently from their English equivalents, the German diphthong [ɔɸ], as in *Fäuste* ['fɔɸstə] "fists," is more closed and more rounded than the English diphthong [ɔɪ] in *foist* [fɔɪst]. Both *eu* and *äu* are pronounced [ɔɸ]: *Leute* ['lɔɸtə] "people," *läute* ['lɔɸtə] "ring."

Occasionally, *e* and *u* appear together as parts of two different elements, as in *beurteilen* "judge"; in such a case, they are of course pronounced separately: [bə'urtaelən].

The singer is cautioned particularly about noting the distinction between the vowels in related words containing *au* and *äu,* such as *Haus* [haos] "house," *Häuser* ['hɔɸzəʁ] "houses."

Exercise 11.3   Contrast *au* and *äu* in the following pairs of related words:

1. lauft   läuft
2. Strauß   Sträuße
3. rauben   Räuber
4. Maus   Mäuse

Exercise 11.4   Pronounce the following words:

1. Täufer, Teufel, feucht, leuchten, Säule
2. Bräutigam, Braut, Frau, Fräulein, zeugen
3. liebäugeln, Efeu, beugen, beunruhigen
4. Streuselkuchen, treuster, Feuer, Löwenbräu

Exercise 11.5   Read the following transcription aloud:

[oː 'kyːləʁ valt, voː 'raoʃəst duː,
ɪn deːm maen 'liːpçən geːt ?

oː ˈviːdɐˌhal, voː ˈlɑoʃəst duː,
deːɐ gɛrn maen liːt fɛɐˈʃteːt ?
ɪm hɛrtsən tiːf dɑː ˈrɑoʃt deːɐ valt,
ɪn deːm maen liːpçən geːt,
ɪn ˈʃmɛrtsən ʃliːf deːɐ ˈviːdɐˌhal,
diː ˈliːdɐ zɪnt fɛɐˈveːt]

Excerpts

1. Streuet ihm, Schwestern,
   Streuet ihm Blumen,
   Bringt ihm knospende Rosen dar.
   Aber euch, Schwestern,
   Grüß' ich mit Wehmut,
   Freudig scheidend aus eurer Schar.

   Frauenliebe und -leben
   Chamisso/Schumann

2. Fleuch, Nachtigall, in grüne Finsternisse,
   Ins Haingesträuch,
   Und spend' im Nest der treuen Gattin Küsse;
   Entfleuch, entfleuch!

   An die Nachtigall
   Hölty/Brahms

3. Sitz nieder, hier dämmert's geheimnisvoll
   Unter den Lindenbäumen,
   Die Nachtigall uns zu Häupten soll
   Von unsren Küssen träumen.

   Ständchen
   Schack/Strauß

4. Die schönen weißen Wolken ziehn dahin
   Durchs tiefe Blau, wie schöne stille Träume,
   Mir ist, als ob ich längst gestorben bin
   Und ziehe selig mit durch ew'ge Räume.

   Feldeinsamkeit
   Allmers/Brahms

Song   Sing the following song, paying special attention to the words containing *eu* and *äu.*

Das Lieben bringt groß' Freud'

Das   Lie - ben bringt groß'___ Freud',   es ___   wis - sen's al - le ___
Ein   Brief - lein schrieb sie___ mir,   ich ___   sollt' treu blei - ben ___
Mein   ei - gen soll sie___ sein,   kei - nem an - dern mehr als ___

Leut'.   Weiß__ mir ein schö - nes Schät - ze - lein mit__
ihr.   Drauf__ schickt' ich ihr ein Sträu - ße - lein, schön__
mein.   So__ le - ben wir in Freud'__ und__ Leid, bis__

zwei schwarz - brau - nen__ Äu - ge - lein, die__ mir, die__
Ros - ma - rin, und__ Nä - ge - lein, sie__ soll, sie__
Gott, der Herr, aus - ein - an - der - scheid't. Dann a - de, dann a -

mir,   die____ mir mein Herz er - freut.
soll,   sie____ soll mein ei - gen__ sein.
de!   Dann a - de, mein Schatz, a - de!

SECTION 4: **Other Vowel Combinations**

In vowel combinations other than those specifically discussed, each member will be pronounced separately: *zuerst* [tsuːˈeːrst] "first," *Poet* [poˈeːt], etc.

Exercise 11.6   Pronounce the following:

1. Kreatur, Diamant, Duell, ideal
2. säen, böig, Poesie

12 The Sounds of *l, r*

SECTION 1: *l, ll*

[l]

n English the sound [l] is articulated with the tongue cupped downward in the middle and the tip resting on the alveolar ridge, as in *fell* [fɛl]. In German, the sound [l] (no difference in transcription) is articulated with the tongue nearly flat and the tip resting against the upper teeth, as in *Fell* [fɛl] "pelt."

Exercise 12.1 Contrast the pronunciation of *l* in the following pairs:

English	*German*
fell	Fell
Helen	hellen
fleck	Fleck
lope	Lob

ll

In speaking, *ll* is pronounced the same as *l*, as in *fällen* ['fɛlən] "to fell"; in singing, *ll* is articulated with greater intensity, resulting in a somewhat extended sound. When *ll* represents parts of two elements, it is markedly lengthened and divided between notes, as in *fühllos* ['fyːlloːs] "unfeeling."

Exercise 12.2 Pronounce the following words:

1. Ball, Lampe, schlau, Schulter, fällen
2. blassen, ablassen, allmächtig, alliebend, Balsam
3. Lieder, Walter, geblichen, vergeblichen, selten
4. wohllautender, Milch, Dolch, solch, gelb, Geld, Klang
5. glich, behaglich, Klavier, tadellos, heillos, bewilligen

Songs Sing the following songs, concentrating on the special articulation of German *l*.

Mein Herz ist voll Lieder

Mein Herz ist voll Lie - der, die See - le voll
Und kä - me mein Schatz mit mir in den

Sang; was ich auch spiel - te ist Froh - sinn, ist Sang; durch
Wald, die Vög - lein al - le, die schwie - gen gar bald, und

Fel - der und Au - en nur ei - ne Me - lo - dei: Mein
lausch - ten auf sei - ne so fro - hen Me - lo - dei'n: Mein

Schatz ist ein Spiel - mann, tan - da - ra - dei, mein
Schatz ist ein Spiel - mann, tan - da - ra - dei, mein

Schatz ist ein Spiel - mann, tan - da - ra - dei.
Schatz ist ein Spiel - mann, tan - da - ra - dei.

Auf der Lüneburger Heide

Auf der Lü - ne - bur - ger Hei - de, in dem
Brü - der laßt die Glä - ser klin - gen, denn der
Und die Hun - de und die bel - len, und die

wun - der - schö - nen Land, ging ich auf und ging ich
Mus - ka - tel - ler Wein wird vom lan - gen Ste - hen
Büch - se und die knallt, ro - te Hir - sche woll'n wir

un - ter, al - ler - lei am Weg ich___ fand.
sau - er, aus - ge - trun - ken muß er___ sein.
ja - gen in dem grü - nen grü - nen___ Wald.

Va - le -

ri, va - le - ra, va - le - ri, va - le - ra, und juch -

hei - ras - sa,___ juch - hei - ras - sa, be - ster Schatz, be - ster Schatz, be - ster

Schatz, be - ster Schatz, denn du weißt es, weißt es ja.

SECTION 2:   *r* (Conclusion), *rr*

Postvocalic *r*

In Chapter 5, we advised the singer to adopt the articulation [ʁ], a vowel-like sound used for *r* in the syllable *-er* and for *r* in final position in certain mono-syllables and prefixes, but to use the single-tap trill [ɾ] for *r* in all other positions. It has no doubt become apparent that *no* singer strictly adheres to this differentiation. However, it has probably become equally apparent that no singer uses *only* the one-tap trill. The English-speaking singer, in part influenced by Italian diction, in part for simplicity's sake, tends to use the trill for all *r*s. This results in an unduly severe sound, especially in the art song. Only by making a somewhat artificial rule for the use of [ɾ] and [ʁ] could we encourage the voice student to develop the use of [ʁ].

Now let us review and expand the guidelines for the use of [ɾ] and [ʁ]. Although [ʁ] *may* be used for any final or preconsonantal *r*, it occurs most frequently, as we saw in Chapter 5, in the following words and elements:

1. the article   *der*
2. the pronouns   *mir*

                         dir

                         er

                         ihr

                         wir

                         wer

3. the prepositions   *für*

                         vor

4. the prefixes   *er-*

                         ver-

                         zer-

5. unstressed   *-er*

The syllable *-er* (but not the prefix *-er*!) is usually pronounced [əʁ] when it is *unstressed* and is final or final before a consonant, as in *aber* ['ɑːbəʁ], *besser* ['bɛsəʁ], *mildert* ['mɪldəʁt], and *hundert* ['hʊndəʁt].

As we have mentioned, the pronunciation of *r* may be [ʁ] in *any* postvocalic position; however, the beginning singer is advised to limit the use of this *r* to the five groups of words listed above.

Otherwise, the pronunciation of *r* is the one-tap trill [ɾ]. The singer is urged to use [ɾ] in the following postvocalic positions: (1) when it appears after a stressed vowel and before a consonant, as in *warten* ['vaɾtən] "wait," *fertig* ['fɛɾtɪç] "finished"; and (2) when it appears finally in most words, for example, *Meer* [meːɾ] "sea," *wahr* [vaːɾ] "true," *fahr'* [faːɾ] "go!"

The choice of articulation for *r* can be of considerable expressive importance in the interpretation of a song. Many singers use the one-tap trill almost exclusively, especially for baroque music and Wagner. Others prefer to use the trill more sparingly, thereby achieving a softer quality. It is recommended that beginning singers adopt the latter approach. This allows for more effective use of the one-tap trill for emphasis and force.

rr

One Element   In one element, *rr* is usually pronounced [ɾ], as in *sperren* [ˈʃpɛɾən] "lock," *dürr* [dʏɾ] "dry," *irrt* [ɪɾt] "errs."

Two Elements   When *rr* represents parts of two elements it is usually pronounced [ʁɾ], as in *Vorrede* [ˈfoːʁˌreːdə] "introduction," *erraten* [ɛʁˈrɑːtən] "guess."

Some singers use an extended trill for *rr* in simple words and compounds as well as for *r* in blends such as *fr* and *tr*. This articulation should be avoided by the beginner.

Exercise 12.3   Pronounce the following words:

1. Torheit, ereilt, beerben, dankerfüllten
2. vereint, wiederholt, Verräter, ehrerbietig, arglos
3. Meisterehre, Meisterregeln, erreicht, surren
4. feuerrot, herrlich, herreiten, Irrtum, Winterreise
5. daran, fortan, hervorrufen, herüberreiten

Exercise 12.4   Transcribe the above words into the IPA.

Songs   Practice the different articulations of *r* by singing the following songs.

Es, es, es und es

Es,	es,	es	und __	es,	es	ist	ein	har	-	ter	Schluß,
Er,	er,	er	und __	er,	Herr	Meis	-	ter	leb'	er	wohl!
Sie,	sie,	sie	und __	sie,	Frau	Meis	-	t'rin	leb'	sie	wohl!
Ihr,	ihr,	ihr	und __	ihr,	ihr	Jung	-	fern	le	- bet	wohl!

weil, weil, weil und __ weil, weil ich aus Frank - furt muß.   Drum __
Er, er, er und __ er, Herr Meis - ter leb' er wohl!   Ich __
Sie, sie, sie und __ sie, Frau Meis - t'rin leb' sie wohl!   Ich __
Ihr, ihr, ihr und __ ihr, ihr Jung - fern le - bet wohl!   Ich __

schlag' ich Frank-furt __ aus dem Sinn und __ wen - de mich, Gott __ weiß wo - hin. Ich
sag's ihm grad' frei __ ins Ge - sicht, sei-ne Ar - beit, die ge - fällt mir nicht. Ich
sag's ihr grad' frei __ ins Ge - sicht, ihr __ Speck und Kraut, das __ schmeckt mir nicht. Ich
wünsch'euchjetzt zu __ gu - ter Letzt ei-nen an - dern, der mein'_ Stell' er-setzt. Ich

will mein Glück pro - bie - ren, mar - schie - ren.
will mein Glück pro - bie - ren, mar - schie - ren.
will mein Glück pro - bie - ren, mar - schie - ren.
will mein Glück pro - bie - ren, mar - schie - ren.

Wohlan, die Zeit ist kommen

Wohl - an, die Zeit ist kom - men, mein Pferd, das muß ge -
In mei - nes Va - ters Gar - ten, da steh'n viel schö - ne
Du glaubst du wärst die Schön - ste wohl auf der gan - zen
Der Kai - ser streit fürs Länd - le, der Her - zog für sein
So - lang' ich leb' auf Er - den, sollst du mein Trim - ple -

sat - telt sein; ich hab' mir's vor - ge - nom - men, ge -
Blum', ja Blum'. Drei Jahr' muß ich noch war - ten, drei
Welt, ja Welt, und auch die An - ge - nehm - ste, ist
Geld, ja Geld, und ich streit' für mein Schätz - le, so -
Tram - ple sein, und wenn ich einst ge - stor - ben bin, so

rit - ten muß es sein!
Jahr' sind bald her - um.
a - ber weit ge - fehlt! Geh du nur hin, ich
lang' es mir ge - fällt.
tram - pelst hin - ter - drein.

hab' mein Teil, ich lieb' dich nur aus Nar – re – tei; oh – ne

dich kann ich wohl le – ben, oh – ne dich kann ich schon sein.

13 The Sounds of *h, j*

SECTION 1: *h*

Silent[1]

n general, *h* is not pronounced after a vowel, unless it begins an element. Specifically, postvocalic *h* is silent: (1) at the end of a word or element, as in *Floh* [floː] "flea," *Gehrock* ['geːˌɾɔk] "coat"; (2) before a consonant, as in *steht* [ʃteːt] "stands"; and (3) before a vowel, as in *gehen* ['geːən] "go." Occasionally singers, even the best, pronounce the *h* in a slow passage in a word like *gehen* ['geːhən]. This is not desirable and sounds affected. However, this situation is not to be confused with that in which *h* begins a new element (see next paragraph "[h]").

[h]

The voiceless glottal fricative [h] is used for *h* at the beginning of a word or element, as in *Hand* [hant] "hand," *gehört* [gəˈhøːɾt] "heard." It is sometimes difficult for the novice to determine whether *h* begins an element: for example, *froher* "merry" is made up of *froh + er* and is pronounced ['froːəʁ], whereas *woher* "whence" is made up of *wo + her* and is pronounced [voˈheːʁ]. The following words, which can prove troublesome, should be memorized:

behende [bəˈhɛndə]	"quick"
woher [voˈheːʁ]	"whence"
daher [dɑˈheːʁ]	"from there"

[1]See Chapter 14 for a discussion of *th*.

Exercise 13.1   Pronounce the following words, observing the rules for pronunciation of *h*:

1. ruhen, ehe, eher, fliehen, Halle, Kindheit
2. hoher, woher, jähes, bisher, einher, wohin
3. geheim, Gehege, gehende, behende, Freiheit
4. Friedhof, gehorchen, Höhe, höhere, Hoheit, allhier
5. wiederholt, dahin, behutsam, abhanden
6. Gotteshaus, Drehorgel, Strohhalm, unbarmherzig

Excerpts

1. Schon krähen die Hähne,
   Und nah ist der Ort.
   . . . .
   Wohl seh' ich, Herrin,
   die Kraft dir schwinden . . .
   Nun wandre, Maria
   Geibel, Heyse/Wolf

2. Fort in die Freiheit!
   dahin gehör' ich,
   Da, wo ich Meister im Haus!
   Die Meistersinger
   Wagner

SECTION 2:   *j*

[j]

In most words, *j* is pronounced as the voiced palatal fricative (or glide) [j], as in *Jammer* [ˈjamɐ] "plaint," *bejahen* [bəˈjɑːən] "affirm," *Major* [maˈjoːr] "major," *Kajak* [ˈkajak] "kayak."

[ʒ]

In a few words of French origin, initial *j* is pronounced as the voiced prepalatal fricative [ʒ]. Learn to recognize the following:

Jalousie [ʒaluˈziː]

Jakett [ʒaˈkɛt]

Jargon [ʒarˈgõ]

Journal [ʒʊrˈnɑːl]

Exercise 13.2   Pronounce the following words:

1. ja, jetzt, jodeln, Majestät, Januar, Jugend
2. Jünger, Journalist, gejagt, Jäger, Jasmin, gejubelt

14 The Sounds of
z, p, t, k, x, qu

SECTION 1:   *z, zz, tz*

[ts]

The letter *z* is pronounced [ts] in all positions: *Zeit* [tsaet] "time," *bezahlen* [bə'tsɑːlən] "pay," *tanzen* ['tantsən] "dance," *Kreuz* [krɔøts] "cross."

zz

In words of Italian origin, *zz* is pronounced [ts]: *Skizze* ['skɪtsə] "sketch," *Intermezzo* [ɪntəʁ'mɛtso].

tz

One Element

When it occurs within one element, *tz* is pronounced the same as *z: setzen* ['zɛtsən] "set," *Schatz* [ʃats] "treasure."

Two Elements

When *t* belongs to one element and *z* to the next, the [t] is prolonged, as in *entzücken* [ɛnt'tsʏkən] "charm."

Exercise 14.1   Pronounce the following words:

1. Platz, Nutzen, trotz, jetzt, Spezerei, gezeigt
2. Zimmer, Frauenzimmer, Zoo, Zürich, zogst
3. verzichten, Wurzel, stürzt, jauchzen, spazieren
4. Walzer, Lenz, Holz, kreuzigten, Geächze

5. Erzengel, erziehen, erzürnt, herzlos, herziehen

6. zitternd, Zephyr, zusammen, herzerschütternd

Excerpts

1. Und nichts zu forschen, nichts zu spähn,
   Und nur zu träumen leicht und lind,
   Der Zeiten Wandel nicht zu sehn,
   Zum zweiten Mal ein Kind!

   O wüßt' ich doch den Weg zurück
   Groth/Brahms

2. Da tanzt den Hochzeitreigen
   Die Herzallerliebste mein.

   Das ist ein Flöten und Geigen
   Heine/Schumann

Tape   Read the following song text onto a tape without stopping the recorder:

Es grünet ein Nußbaum vor dem Haus,
Duftig,
Luftig
Breitet er blättrig die Äste aus.

Viel liebliche Blüten stehen dran;
Linde
Winde
Kommen, sie herzlich zu umfahn.

Es flüstern je zwei zu zwei gepaart,
Neigend,
Beugend
Zierlich zum Kusse die Häuptchen zart.

Sie flüstern von einem Mägdlein, das
Dächte
Nächte
Tagelang, wußte, ach, selber nicht was.

Sie flüstern, wer mag verstehn so gar
Leise
Weise?
Flüstern von Bräut'gam und nächstem Jahr.

Das Mägdlein horchet, es rauscht im Baum;
Sehnend,
Wähnend
Sinkt es lächelnd in Schlaf und Traum.

Der Nußbaum
Mosen/Schumann

Song   Sing the following song, concentrating on the pronunciation of *z*.

Morgen muß ich fort

Mor - gen muß ich fort von hier und muß Ab - schied
Wenn zwei gu - te Freun - de sind, die ein - an - der
Küs - set dir ein Lüf - te - lein Wan - gen o - der

neh - men; o du al - ler - schön - ste Zier, Schei - den, das_____ bringt
ken - nen, Sonn' und Mond be - we - gen sich, e - he sie_____ sich
Hän - de, den - ke, daß es Seuf - zer sind, die ich zu_____ dir

Grä - men. Da ich dich so treu ge - liebt
tren - nen. Noch viel grö - ßer ist der Schmerz,
sen - de; tau - send schick' ich täg - lich aus,

ü - ber al - le Ma - ßen,   soll ich dich ver -
wenn ein treu ver - lieb - tes Herz   in die Frem - de
die da we - hen um dein Haus,   weil ich dein ge -

las - sen,___ sol ich___ dich ver las - sen.
zie - het,___ in die___ Frem - de zie - het.
den - ke,___ weil ich___ dein ge - den - ke.

SECTION 2:   *p, pp, pf, ps, ph*

[p]

As in English, *p* represents the voiceless bilabial stop [p], as in *Pein* [paen] "pain," *geprahlt* [gəˈprɑːlt] "boasted."

pp

[p]

Since *pp* does not normally occur at the junction of two elements in a compound, we can say that it is usually pronounced the same as *p*, as in *Lippe* [ˈlɪpə] "lip," *Suppe* [ˈzʊpə] "soup," *schnappt* [ʃnapt] "snaps." Some feel that the sound should be extended slightly when it appears between vowels.

pf

[pf]

The combination *pf* always represents the affricate [pf]. When it occurs at the beginning of a word or element, as in *Pfad* [pfɑːt] "path," *gepfiffen* [gə'pfɪfən] "whistled," it is launched as a unit on the same note. If it occurs intervocalically in a noncompound word such as *Apfel* ['apfəl] "apple," the [p] is usually begun on one beat and released as [f] on the next. The singer must be careful to sound the [p] in this combination.

Exercise 14.2   Pronounce:

    1. Pfeife, Pferd, Pflanze

    2. tapfer, Gipfel, klopfen

ps
[ps]

The combination *ps* is always pronounced [ps], even at the beginning of a word, as in *Psalm* [psalm].

ph
[f]

The combination *ph* is normally pronounced [f], as in *Phrase* ['frɑːzə].

Exercise 14.3   Pronounce:

    1. Palme, Treppe, Doppelgänger, Pinie, Puppe

    2. Pfeil, Pflaume, Schnaps, Phantasie, prächtig

    3. Posten, Pfosten, Pfriem, verpflichten, schlüpfen

    4. gepflückt, Psyche, Prophet, Phönix, Pappeln, Sphären

Excerpt   1. Die Trommel gerühret, das Pfeifchen gespielt!
    Mein Liebster gewaffnet dem Haufen befiehlt,
    Die Lanze hoch führet, die Leute regieret.
    Wie klopft mir das Herz! Wie wallt mir das Blut!
       Die Trommel gerühret
       Goethe/Beethoven

    2. Mit Tritten wie Tritte der Elfen so sacht,
    Um über die Blumen zu hüpfen,
    Flieg leicht hinaus in die Mondscheinnacht,
    Zu mir in den Garten zu schlüpfen.
       Ständchen
       Schack/Strauß

    3. Flieg her zum Krippelein,
    Flieg her, gefiedert Schwesterlein,
    Blas an den feinen Psalterlein,
    Sing, Nachtigall, gar fein!
       Wach, Nachtigall, wach auf!
       Folk Song

Song   Sing the following song, concentrating on the pronunciation of *p* and its combinations.

Der Apfel ist nicht gleich am Baum

Der Ap - fel ist nicht gleich___ am Baum. Da
Dann wa - ren Blät - ter grün___ an grün und
Der Herbst, der macht die Blät - ter steif. Der
Und was bei Sonn' und Him - mel war, er -

war___ erst lau - ter Blü - te. Da war erst lau - ter
grün___ an grün nur Blä - ter. Die Am - sel nach___ des
Som - mer muß sich pak - ken. Hei, daß ich auf___ dem
quickt___ nun Mund und Ma - gen, und macht die Au - gen

Blü - ten - schaum. Da war erst lau - ter
Ta - ges Müh'n, sie sang ihr A - bend -
Fin - ger pfeif': da sind die er - sten
hell___ und klar. So run - det sich das

Früh - lings - traum und lau - ter Lieb'___ und Gü - te.
lied___ gar kühn. Und auch bei Re - gen - wet - ter.
Äp - fel reif, und ha - ben ro - te Bak - ken.
Ap - fel - jahr. Und mehr ist nicht___ zu sa - gen.

SECTION 3:   *t, tt, th, tsch, ti*

[t]

As in English, *t* usually represents the voiceless alveolar stop [t], as in *Tal* [tɑːl] "valley," *beten* ['beːtən] "pray."

tt

One Element

When it occurs in one element, as in *Betten* ['bɛtən] "beds," *Fittich* ['fɪtɪç] "wing," *tt* is usually pronounced [t].

Two Elements

When *tt* represents parts of two elements, as in *Bettag* ['beːt̩tɑːk] "day of prayer," it is pronounced [tt].

th

One Element

When *th* does not represent parts of different elements, it is pronounced [t]. In modern German, *th* appears in only a few words which are not compounds, for example *Theater* [te'ɑːtɐ], *Apotheke* [apo'teːkə].

Musical scores often keep the archaic spelling *th* for *t*, as in *Rath* [ɾɑːt] (modern: *Rat*) "counsel," *Theil* [tael] (modern: *Teil*) "part."

Two Elements

In a number of words, *th* represents parts of two elements in a compound. Since in this case the second element begins with *h,* it is pronounced, as in *Rathaus* ['ɾɑːt̩hɑos] "town hall."

tsch

[t ʃ]

The combination *tsch* represents the affricate [tʃ], as in *Deutsch* [dɔøtʃ] "German."

ti

[tsi]

In a number of words of Latin origin, *ti* is pronounced [tsɪ]. The only members of this group which might be of interest to the singer are those containing the syllable *-tion,* as in *Nation* [na'tsɪoːn], *Aktion* [ak'tsɪoːn].

Exercise 14.4   Pronounce the following words, observing the rules for the pronunciation of *t* and its combinations:

1. Tat, Atem, Schatten, Retter, Hüte, Hütte
2. Auktion, Thema, rotglühend, Therese, dritte
3. enttäuschen, muthig, Thränen, dorthin, Guttat
4. entrauschen, welthellsichtig, Thor, Festtag, flattern
5. Blüthendampfe, Posthorn, Beethoven, plätschern
6. Wehmutsstrahlen, Götter, Hauptton, weither, Walther
7. bereithalten, Bettag, Bretter, bitter, rutschen
8. Funktion, Gasthaus, Peitsche, getheilt, enthält
9. Gasthof, Nation, Wehmuthsthränen, Liebeston, Zither
10. gutherzig, mitreisen, Apostel, Ästhetik
11. Äther, liebestrunken, trösten, Elisabeth, Urtheil

Excerpts   Read the following excerpts aloud:

1. So war es mein Kuß,
   Der welthellsichtig dich machte?
   Mein volles Liebesumfangen
   läßt dich dann Gottheit erlangen.
      Parsifal
      Wagner

2. Noch war kein Tag, wo du und ich
   Nicht theilten unsre Sorgen.
   Auch waren sie für dich und mich
   Getheilt leicht zu ertragen;
   Du tröstetest im Kummer mich,
   Ich weint' in deine Klagen . . .
      Ich liebe dich
      Herossee/Beethoven

3. All' solch' dein' Güt' wir preisen,
   Vater ins Himmelsthron,
   Die du uns thust beweisen,
   durch Christum, deinen Sohn,
   und bitten ferner dich:
   gieb uns ein friedlich's Jahre,
   für allem Leid bewahre
   und nähr' uns mildiglich.
      Zeuch ein zu deinen Toren
      Bach

SECTION 4:   *k, kn, ck, kk*

[k]

The letter *k* is always pronounced [k], as in *kaum* [kɑom] "hardly," *krumm* [krʊm] "crooked," *beklagen* [bəˈklɑːgən] "complain."

kn

[k n]

Even at the beginning of an element, the *k* is pronounced in the combination *kn,* as in *Knabe* [ˈknɑːbə] "lad," *geknüpft* [gəˈknʏpft] "knotted."

ck

[k]

The combination *ck* is pronounced [k], as in *nicken* [ˈnɪkən] "nod," *steckt* [ʃtɛkt] "sticks." When a word must be divided at *ck* in a musical score, it is spelled *k-k*: *lok-ki-gen* = *lockigen* "curly."

kk

One Element

The double consonant *kk* appears in only a few words which are not compounds. In these words, which are usually of foreign origin, *kk* is pronounced [k], for example, in *Akkord* [aˈkɔrt] "chord."

Two Elements

Usually, *kk* represents parts of two elements, often in the form *ckk,* and is therefore pronounced as an extended [kk], as in *Rückkehr* [ˈrʏkˌkeːr] "return."

Exercise 14.5 Pronounce:

1. Kahn, Kinn, kühl, Kur, verkaufen
2. Bäcker, versteckte, frohlocken, Hecken, Backofen
3. eklig, Knopf, akkurat, Schmuckkasten
4. Pauke, Onkel, Birke, Schurke, Schalk
5. Waldecke, entrückte, Droschke, glücklich, zurückkehren
6. Edikt, Kerker, kräftig, Sklave, Knackwurst
7. knüpfen, geknallt, Knie, Knospe, verkniffen
8. gekleidet, Kümmel, Klee, geklebt, klopft, Häkchen

Excerpts

1. Knusper, knusper, Knäuschen,
   Wer knuspert mir am Häuschen.
   Hänsel und Gretel
   Humperdinck

2. Petrus, der nicht denkt zurück,
   Seinen Gott verneinet,
   Der doch auf ein'n ernsten Blick
   Bitterlichen weinet:
   Jesu, blicke mich auch an,

Wenn ich nicht will büßen;
Wenn ich Böses hab' gethan,
Rühre mein Gewissen.

Jesu Leiden, Pein und Tod
Bach

Song   Sing the following song, paying attention to the words containing *k* and its combinations.

Es wohnt ein Kaiser an dem Rhein

1. Es wohnt ein Kai - ser an dem Rhein, der hat drei schö - ne Töch - ter -
2. Die er - ste wollt' die reich - ste sein, die zwei - te zog ins Klo - ster
3. Die drit - te zog ins frem - de Land, da war sie fremd und un - be -
4. Bei ei - ner Wir - tin klopft sie an, da ward die Tür ihr auf - ge -
5. Wer steht da drau - ßen vor der Tür? Eine ar - me Dienst - magd steht da -
6. So ei - ne Dienst - magd brauch' ich nicht, die a - bends vor den Tü - ren
7. Mein Vater ist Kai - ser an dem Rhein, und ich bin Kai - sers Töch - ter -
8. Das konnt'st du mir schon e - her sagen, ge - stick - te Klei - der konnt'st du
9. Und als sie nun ge - stor - ben war, drei Lil - ien wuch - sen auf ih - rem

1. lein, Töch - ter - lein, der hat drei schö - ne Töch - ter - lein.
2. ein, Klo - ster ein, die zwei - te zog ins Klo - ster ein.
3. kannt, un - be - kannt, da war sie fremd und un - be - kannt.
4. tan, auf - ge - tan, da ward die Tür ihr auf - ge - tan.
5. für, steht da - für, eine ar - me Dienst - magd steht da - für.
6. liegt, Tü - ren liegt, die a - bends vor den Tü - ren liegt.
7. lein, Töch - ter - lein, und ich bin Kai - sers Töch - ter - lein.
8. tragen, konnt'st du tragen, ge - stick - te Klei - der konnt'st du tragen.
9. Grab, ih - rem Grab, drei Lil - ien wuch - sen auf ihr - rem Grab.

SECTION 5:   *x*

[ks]

The letter *x* is pronounced [ks], as in *Hexe* [ˈhɛksə] "witch," *Nixe* [ˈnɪksə] "nymph."

SECTION 6:   *qu*

[kv]

The combination *qu* is pronounced [kv], as in *Quarz* [kvaɾts].

Exercise 14.6   Pronounce:

Qual
Qualität
qualmen
einquartieren
entquellen

Exercise 14.7   Read the following transcription aloud:

[alˈnɛçtlɪç ̩ɪm ˈtʁɑomə zeː ̩ɪç dɪç,
̩ʊnt ˈzeːə dɪç ˈfʁɔøntlɪç ˈgʁyːsən,
̩ʊnt lɑot ̩ɑofˌvaenənt ʃtʏɾts ̩ɪç mɪç
tsuː ˈdaenən ˈzyːsən ˈfyːsən.

duː ˈziːəst mɪç ̩an ˈveːˌmyːtɪklɪç
̩ʊnt ˈʃʏtəlst das ˈblɔndə ˈkœpfçən;
̩ɑos ˈdaenən ̩ɑogən ˈʃlaeçən zɪç
diː ˈpɛɾlənˌtʁeːnənˌtʁœpfçən.

duː zɑːkst miːʁ ˈhaemlɪç ̩aen ˈlaezəs vɔɾt
̩ʊnt giːpst miːʁ deːn ʃtʁɑos fɔn tsyˈpʁɛsən.
̩ɪç ˈvaχə ̩ɑof, ̩ʊnt deːʁ ʃtʁɑos ̩ɪst fɔɾt,
̩ʊnts vɔɾt hɑːp ̩ɪç fɛʁˈgɛsən].

Excerpt   Read the following excerpt aloud:

Das heiße Sündenblut entquillt,
ewig erneut aus des Sehnens Quelle.
Parsifal
Wagner

Song   Sing the following song.

Hänsel und Gretel

Hän - sel und Gre - tel ver - lie - fen sich im Wald.
Hu, hu, da schaut ei - ne al - te He - xe raus!
Doch als die He - xe zum O - fen schaut hin - ein,

Es war so fin - ster und auch so grim - mig kalt. Sie
Lock - te die Kin - der ins Pfef - fer - ku - chen - haus. Sie
ward sie ge - sto - ßen vom Hans und Gre - te - lein. Die

ka - men an ein Häus - chen von Pfef - fer - ku - chen fein:
stell - te sich gar freund - lich o Hän - sel, wel - che Not!
He - xe muß - te bra - ten, die Kin - der geh'n nach Haus.

Wer mag der Herr wohl von die - sem Häus - chen sein?
Ihn wollt' die bra - ten im O - fen braun wie Brot.
Nun ist das Mär - chen von Hans und Gre - tel aus.

15 The Sounds of c[1]

SECTION 1:   *c*

The letter *c* rarely occurs before a vowel in modern German. It does, however, occur in archaic spellings, which are fairly commonly used in song texts.

[ts]

Before a front vowel, *c* is pronounced [ts]: *Cäsar* ['tsɛːzɑɾ] "Caesar," *cis* [tsɪs] "C-sharp," *ces* [tsɛs] "C-flat."[2]

[k]

Before a back vowel, *c* is pronounced [k]: *Café* [ka'feː], *Cousin* [ku'zɛ̃].

SECTION 2:   *ch* (Conclusion)

[χ]

In Chapter 5, it was pointed out that *ch* is regularly pronounced as the voiceless velar fricative [χ] after *a, o, u,* and *au: Bach* [baχ], *doch* [dɔχ].

---

[1]See Chapter 14 for *ck*.
[2]In *Cello, Cembalo, c* is pronounced [tʃ].

[ç]

1. After all other vowels and after consonants, *ch* is pronounced as the voiceless palatal fricative [ç]. It is especially important to be aware of this distinction in related forms with and without umlaut: *Buch* [buːχ] "book," *Bücher* ['byːçɐʁ] "books"; *lachen* ['laχən] "laugh," *lächerlich* ['lɛçɐʁlɪç] "ridiculous."

2. At the beginning of a few words, *ch* is [ç], for example:

Cherub ['çeːɾʊp]	cherub
China ['çiːnɑ]	China

(also frequently pronounced with [k]: ['keːɾʊp], ['kiːnɑ])

[k]

In a number of words of Greek origin, the spelling *ch* represents the pronunciation [k]; learn to recognize the following:

Charakter	melancholisch
Chor	Orchester
Choral	Chronik
Christ	

Exercise 15.1   Pronounce:

1. verachten, verächtlich, Buch, Bücher, durchaus
2. Loch, Löcher, hoch, höchste, Kirchhof
3. Flucht, flüchtig, Sprache, Gespräch, Fichte
4. flechten, flocht, sprechen, sprach, gesprochen
5. Gedächtnis, dachte, Geschichte, dicht, Psyche
6. mißachten, Macht, mächtig, bezeichnet, Dolch
7. durchschleichen, Melancholie, Eiche, Cabaret, Cäcilie
8. Drache, christlich, chaotisch, Chor, Echo
9. Rauch, räuchern, chinesisch, mochte, möchte

Excerpts   Read the following excerpts aloud:

1. Ach! denkt das Veilchen, wär' ich nur
   Die schönste Blume der Natur,
   Ach! nur ein kleines Weilchen,
   Bis mich das Liebchen abgepflückt
   Und an dem Busen matt gedrückt,
   Ach nur, ach nur
   Ein Viertelstündchen lang!
   Ach, aber ach! das Mädchen kam

Und nicht in acht das Veilchen nahm,
Ertrat das arme Veilchen.

Das Veilchen
Goethe/Mozart

2. Ich möchte nicht mehr leben,
   Möcht' augenblicks verderben,
   Und möchte doch auch leben
   Für dich, mit dir, und nimmer, nimmer sterben.
   Ach, rede, sprich ein Wort nur,
   Ein einziges, ein klares . . .

Nicht mehr zu dir zu gehen
Daumer/Brahms

Tape   Read the following song text onto a tape without stopping the recorder:

Wehe, Lüftchen, lind und lieblich
Um die Wange der Geliebten
Spiele zart in ihrer Locke,
Eile nicht, hinweg zu fliehn!

Tut sie dann vielleicht die Frage,
Wie es um mich Armen stehe;
Sprich: "Unendlich war sein Wehe,
Höchst bedenklich seine Lage;

Aber jetzo kann er hoffen,
Wieder herrlich aufzuleben,
Denn du, Holde, Denkst an ihn."

Botschaft
Daumer (after Hafis)/Brahms

Songs   Sing the following songs, paying special attention to the pronunciation of *ch*.

Freut euch des Lebens

Lämp - chen glüht, pflük - ket___ die Ro - se,
Lämp - chen glüht, pflük - ket___ die Ro - se,
Lämp - chen glüht, pflük - ket___ die Ro - se,
Lämp - chen glüht, pflük - ket___ die Ro - se,

Fine

eh' sie___ ver - blüht! ___ Man schafft so gern___ sich
eh' sie___ ver - blüht! ___ Wer Red - lich - keit___ und
eh' sie___ ver - blüht! ___ Und wenn der Pfad___ sich
eh' sie___ ver - blüht! ___ Sie ist des Le - bens

Sorg' und Müh', sucht Dor - nen auf und fin - det sie und
Treu - e liebt und gern dem är - mern Bru - der gibt, da
furcht - bar engt und Miß - ge - schick sich plagt und drängt
schön - stes Band, schlingt Brü - der trau - lich Hand in Hand, so

D.C. al Fine

läßt das Veil - chen un - be - merkt, das uns am We - ge blüht.
sie - delt sich Zu - frie - den - heit so ger - ne bei ihm ein.
reicht die Freund-schaft schwes - ter - lich dem Red - li - chen die Hand.
wallt man froh, so wallt man leicht ins bess' - re Va - ter - land.

Brüderchen, komm, tanz mit mir

1. Brü - der - chen, komm, tanz mit mir, bei - de Händ - chen reich' ich dir,
2. Tan - zen soll ich ar - mer Wicht? Gre - tel, nein, das kann ich nicht!
3. Mit dem Köpf-chen nick, nick, nick, mit dem Finger - chen tick, tick, tick.
4. Ei, das hast du fein ge - macht, ei, das hätt' ich nicht ge - dacht.
5. Mit den Händ-chen klapp, klapp, klapp, mit den Füß - chen trapp, trapp, trapp.

1. ein - mal hin, ein - mal her, rings - her - um, das ist nicht schwer.
2. Drum zeig mir, wie es Brauch, daß ich tan - zen ler - ne auch.
3. Ein - mal hin, ein - mal her, rings - her - um, das ist nicht schwer.
4. Seht mir doch den Hansl an, wie der Hans - l tan - zen kann!
5. Ein - mal hin, ein - mal her, rings - her - um, das ist nicht schwer.

SECTION 3:   *chs*

One Element

When *chs* occurs within one element, it is pronounced [ks], as in *wachsen* ['vaksən] "grow."

Since it can be seen from the next section, "Two Elements," that a rather sizable number of forms can be derived in which *chs* is *not* pronounced [ks], the singer should become familiar with some common words containing *chs* within one element:

Achse	"axle"	Sachsen	"Saxony"
Achsel	"shoulder"	sechs	"six"
Büchse	"rifle, box"	Wachs	"wax"
Dachs	"badger"	wachsen	"grow"
Deichsel	"shaft"	du wächst	"you grow"
Drechsler	"turner"	er wächst	"he grows"
Fuchs	"fox"	er wuchs	"he grew"
Fuchsie	"fuchsia"	wechseln	"change"
Gewächs	"growth"	Weichsel	kind of cherry
Lachs	"salmon"		
Luchs	"lynx"		
Ochse	"ox"		

Two Elements

When *ch* belongs to one element and *s* to the next, each must of course be pronounced with its element and in accordance with the rules for *ch* and *s* respectively.

1. *ch* + verb ending *-st*:

   du lachst [laχst] "you laugh" < *lachen*

   du weichst [vaeçst] "you retreat" < *weichen*

2. *ch* + noun ending *-s*:

   des Bachs [baχs] "of the brook" < *Bach*

   des Blechs [blεçs] "of the metal" < *Blech*

3. *ch* + superlative suffix *-st*:

   höchst [hø:çst] "highest"

   nächst- [nε:çst] "nearest, next"

   herrlichsten ['hεɾlıçstən] "most splendid"

4. Compounds:

   durchspielen ['dʊɾçʃpi:lən] "play through"

   Lochsäge ['lɔχˌzε:gə] "keyhole saw"

Exercise 15.2   Pronounce:

1. sechs, wechselt, wachsen, Fuchs, Buchs
2. erbleichst, Deichsel, Lachs, Bachs, lachst
3. sprichst, brichst, Gewächs, Gesprächs
4. Büchse, herrlichste, siegreichsten, Buchstabe
5. weichst, Weichsel, Königreichs, lieblichsten
6. huldreichstes, höchsten, nächste, wächst
7. Gebrauchs, Gefährlichsten, durchsetzen, wachsam

Exercise 15.3   Transcribe the words in Exercise 15.2 into the IPA.

16 The Sounds of *w, v, f*

SECTION 1: *w*

The letter *w* is almost always pronounced [v], as in *Wein* [vaen] "wine," *zwei* [tsvae] "two."

Exercise 16.1   Pronounce:

1. woher, gewohnt, entzwei, zwanzig, zwölf

2. schwarz, schwingen, wegwerfen, Löwe, wogten

3. Juwel, jeweils, Möwe, bewegt, beschwört

Excerpts   Read the following excerpts aloud:

1. Jeder wird sich glücklich scheinen,
   Wenn mein Bild vor ihm erscheint,
   Eine Träne wird er weinen,
   Und ich weiß nicht, was er weint.
   Harfenspieler
   Goethe/Wolf

2. O wer sehen könnte, welche Bilder
   Hinter dieser Stirne, diesen schwarzen
   Wimpern sich in sanftem Wechsel malen!
   Schlafendes Jesuskind
   Mörike/Wolf

3. Ach, es entschwindet mit tauigem Flügel
   Mir auf den wiegenden Wellen die Zeit.
   Morgen entschwindet mit schimmerndem Flügel
   Wieder wie gestern und heute die Zeit,
   Bis ich auf höherem strahlendem Flügel
   Selber entschwinde der wechselnden Zeit.
   Lied auf dem Wasser zu singen
   Stolberg/Schubert

Song   Sing the following song, concentrating on the pronunciation of *w* (note that *v* is usually pronounced [f]).

Morgen will mein Schatz verreisen

Mor - gen will mein Schatz ver - rei - sen,   Ab - schied neh - men mit Ge -
Sa - ßen da zwei Tur - tel - tau - ben,   sa - ßen wohl auf grü - nem
Laub und Gras, das mag ver - wel - ken,   a - ber uns - re Lie - be
Ei - ne Schwal - be macht kein'n Som - mer,   ob sie gleich die er - ste

walt.   Drau - ßen sin - gen schon die Vö - gel,   sin - gen schon die
Ast.   Wo sich zwei ver - lieb - te schei - den,   zwei ver - lieb - te
nicht.   Du kommst mir aus mei - nen Au - gen,   mir aus mei - nen
ist;   und mein Lieb - chen macht mir Kum - mer,   Lieb - chen macht mir

Vö - gel in dem grü - nen, grü - nen Wald.
schei - den, da ver - wel - ken Laub und Gras.
Au - gen, a - ber aus dem Her - zen nicht.   Denn es fällt mir so schwer aus der
Kum - mer, ob sie gleich die Schön - ste ist.

Hei - mat zu geh'n, wenn die Hoff - nung nicht wär' auf ein

Wie - der, Wie - der-sehn, le - be wohl, le - be wohl, le - be

wohl, le - be wohl, le - be wohl, auf Wie - der___ sehn!

SECTION 2:   *v*

[f]

In words of Germanic origin, *v* is pronounced [f], as in *viel* [fiːl] "much,"
Bevölkerung [bəˈfœlkərʊŋ] "population." It is also pronounced [f] in

Vers [fɛɾs][1]	"verse"
Veilchen [ˈfaelçən]	"violet"
Vogt [foːkt]	"warden, governor"

[1]The pronunciation [vɛɾs] is also heard.

[v]

In most words of foreign origin, *v* is pronounced [v] before a vowel: *Vase* ['vɑːzə], *Klavier* [klaˈviːr], *braver* ['brɑːvəʁ][2]. However, like *b, d, g, s*, it becomes unvoiced in final position or before a consonant: *brav* [brɑːf], *bravster* ['brɑːfstəʁ].

Exercise 16.2   Pronounce:

1. Vater, völlig, vervollständigen, Violine, vom

2. brave, brav, nervös, Nerv, Villa, Venus

3. Klavier, Frevel, Frevler, Provinz, November

4. Vetter, Novelle, Viola, vielleicht, Sklave

5. bevor, davon, Virtuose, Veilchen, Vers, verweht

6. Levkoje, Tonverschiebung, Pulver, privat, Universität

Excerpt   Read the following excerpt aloud:

So wandelt froh auf Gottes Wegen,
Und was ihr thut, das thut getreu!
Verdienet eures Gottes Segen,
Denn der ist alle Morgen neu:
Denn welcher seine Zuversicht
Auf Gott setzt, den verläßt er nicht.

> *Wer nur den lieben Gott läßt walten*
> Bach

Song   Sing the following song, concentrating on the pronunciation of *v*.

Wieder einmal ausgeflogen

Wie - der ein - mal aus - ge - flo - gen, wie - der ein - mal heim - ge -
Wird uns wie - der wohl ver - ei - nen, fri - scher Ost und fri - scher
Im - mer schwe - rer wird das Päck - chen, kaum noch trägt es sich al -
Und an sei - nes Hau - ses Schwel - le wird ein je - der fest ge -

[2]The pronunciation ['brɑːfəʁ] is also heard.

kehrt,   fand   ich   doch   die   al - ten   Freun - de,   fand   ich
West?   Auch   die   lo - se - sten   der   Vö - gel,   auch   die
lein,   und   in   im - mer   eng' - re   Fes - seln,   und   in
bannt,   a - ber   Lie - bes - fä - den   spin - nen,   a - ber

doch die al - ten Freun - de   und die   Her - zen   un - ver - sehrt.
lo - se - sten der Vö - gel   tra - gen   all - ge - mach zu   Nest.
im - mer eng' - re Fes - seln   schlin - get   uns   die   Hei - mat   ein.
Lie - bes - fä - den spin - nen   heim - lich   sich   von   Land zu   Land.

SECTION 3:   *f, ff*

The letter *f* is always pronounced [f] as in *fein* [faen] "fine," *Brief* [briːf] "letter," *gefragt* [gəˈfrɑːkt] "asked."

ff

One Element

When *ff* occurs within one element, it is pronounced [f], as in *treffen* [ˈtrɛfən] "meet," *trifft* [trɪft] "meets."

Two Elements

Occasionally, *ff* constitutes parts of two elements, in which case the sound is prolonged, as in *auffahren* [ˈaofˌfɑːrən] "rise."

Exercise 16.3   Pronounce:

1. Fuge, fällen, führen, Efeu, rufen
2. Neffe, Ofen, offen, Öfen, öffnen

3. schlafe, schlaffe, aufliegen, auffliegen, auffallen

4. Stiefvater, aufragen, befragen, schroff, pfiff

5. Pfeife, Haufen, häufig, schafft, Schaft, verblüfft

Tape   Read the following song text onto a tape without stopping the recorder:

Wie Melodien zieht es mir leise durch den Sinn,
Wie Frühlingsblumen blüht es und schwebt wie Duft dahin.
Doch kommt das Wort und faßt es und führt es vor das Aug',
Wie Nebelgrau erblaßt es und schwindet wie ein Hauch.
Und dennoch ruht im Reime verborgen wohl ein Duft,
Den mild aus stillem Keime ein feuchtes Auge ruft.

> *Wie Melodien zieht es mir*
> *Groth/Brahms*

17 The Sounds of *m, n*

SECTION 1:   *m, mm*

The letter *m* is pronounced [m], as in *mein* [maen], "my," *kamen* [ˈkɑːmən] "came."

mm

One Element

In speaking, *mm* in one element is pronounced [m], as in *Flamme* [ˈflame] "flame," *flammt* [flamt] "flames." In singing, *mm* is articulated with greater intensity, resulting in a somewhat extended sound.

Two Elements

In a few instances, *mm* represents parts of two elements and the pronunciation is extended, as in *ummalen* [ˈʊmˌmɑːlən] "repaint." Since many coaches recommend beginning the articulation of *m* on one note and concluding it on the next, there is little effective difference in singing between [m] and [mm]. The same applies to [n] and [nn].

Excerpt

Read the following excerpt aloud:

Mach auf, mach auf, doch leise, mein Kind,
Um keinen vom Schlummer zu wecken;
Kaum murmelt der Bach, kaum zittert im Wind
Ein Blatt an den Büschen und Hecken.
Drum leise, mein Mädchen, daß nichts sich regt,
Nur leise die Hand auf die Klinke gelegt.

Ständchen
Schack/Strauß

SECTION 2:   *n, nn, ng, nk*

As in English, the letter *n* is pronounced as the voiced alveolar nasal [n]: *nein* [naen] "no," *blind* [blɪnt] "blind."

149

nn

One Element Usually, *nn* belongs to one element and is pronounced [n], as in *Tanne* ['tanə] "fir," *nennt* [nɛnt] "calls."

Two Elements Since several prefixes end in *n*, *nn* sometimes represents parts of two elements, as in *annehmen* ['anˌneːmən] "assume," *hinnehmen* ['hɪnˌneːmən] "accept." Although *nn* is properly transcribed [nn] in these cases, there may be little difference in pronunciation between [n] and [nn], depending on style (see "Section 1" above).

ng

One Element When *ng* occurs within one element it is always pronounced [ŋ], as in *Finger* ['fɪŋəʁ] "finger," *Hunger* ['hʊŋəʁ] "hunger," *Klang* [klaŋ] "sound."

Two Elements When *n* and *g* represent parts of two elements, they are pronounced as [n] + [g], as in *angehen* ['anˌgeːən] "concern," *hingehen* ['hɪnˌgeːən] "go there."

nk

One Element When *nk* occurs within one element it is always pronounced [ŋk], as in *dunkel* ['dʊŋkəl] "dark," *Dank* [daŋk] "thanks."

Two Elements When *n* and *k* belong to different elements, they are pronounced as [n] + [k], as in *ankommen* ['anˌkɔmən] "arrive," *unklar* ['ʊnˌklaːr] "unclear."

Exercise 17.1 Pronounce:

1. Ring, Doppelgänger, Meistersänger, danken, denken
2. Hingabe, hing, hingehören, hinken, hinkommen
3. angelehnt, Engel, dringlich, grimmig, kommen
4. jüngrem, Haingesträuch, Frühlingsabendrot, ringsum
5. Engelszungen, Angebinde, Tränenahnung, hinnen, herannahen
6. Mondscheinnacht, kennen, ungeleitet, unnütz, Brunnen
7. Junggeselle, Gesangstunde, Gemeingut, Jammer
8. annehmen, dennoch, angenommen, Funktion, Spengler
9. Götterfunken, klangreich, klingen, Tonkunst, Junker-Unkraut
10. Drangsal, empfange, englisch, entlanggehen, Unglück

Exercise 17.2 Read the following transcription aloud:

[deːʁ toːt das ˌɪst diː ˈkyːlə naχt
das ˈleːbən ˌɪst deːʁ ˈʃvyːlə taːk

ɛs ˈduŋkəlt ʃoːn mɪç ˈʃlɛːfəʁt
deːʁ taːk hat mɪç myːt gəˈmaχt
ˈyːbəʁ maen bɛt ɛʁˈheːpt zɪç aen baom
dʀɪn zɪŋt di ˈjuŋə ˈnaχtɪgal
ziː zɪŋt fɔn ˈlaotəʁ ˈliːbə
ɪç høːr ‖ɛs zoːˈgaːr ‖ɪm traom]

Excerpts   Read the following excerpts aloud:

1. Wie im Morgenglanze du rings mich anglühst,
   Frühling, Geliebter!
   Ganymed
   Goethe/Schubert

2. Dein Angesicht, so lieb und schön,
   Das hab' ich jüngst im Traum gesehn,
   Es ist so mild und engelgleich,
   Und doch so bleich, so schmerzenreich.
   Dein Angesicht
   Heine/Schumann

Tape   Read the following song text onto a tape without stopping the recorder:

Holder klingt der Vogelsang,
Wenn die Engelreine,
Die mein Jünglingsherz bezwang,
Wandelt durch die Haine.

Röter blühet Tal und Au,
Grüner wird der Rasen,
Wo die Finger meiner Frau
Maienblumen lasen.

Ohne sie ist alles tot,
Welk sind Blüt' und Kräuter;
Und kein Frühlingsabendrot
Dünkt mir schön und heiter.

Traute, minnigliche Frau
Wollest nimmer fliehen,
Daß mein Herz gleich dieser Au,
Mög' in Wonne blühen.
   Minnelied
   Hölty/Brahms

Songs   Sing the following songs, concentrating on the sounds of *m* and *n*.

Ade, zur guten Nacht

A - de zur gu - ten Nacht, jetzt ist der Schluß ge - macht, daß
Es trau - ern Berg und Tal, wo ich viel tau - send - mal bin
Das Brünn - lein rinnt und rauscht wohl un - term Hol - der - strauch, da
Die Mäd - chen in der Welt sind fal - scher als das Geld mit

ich muß schei - den. Im Som - mer wächst der Klee, im
drü - ber gan - gen. Das hat dei - ne Schön - heit ge - macht, hat
wir ge - ses - sen. So man - chen Glok - ken - schlag, wo
ih - rem Lie - ben. A - de zur gu - ten Nacht, jetzt

Win - ter schneit's den Schnee: da komm' ich wie - der.
mich zum Lie - ben ge - bracht mit gro - ßem Ver - lan - gen.
Herz bei Her - zen lag, das hast ver - ges - sen.
ist der Schluß ge - macht, daß ich muß schei - den.

O Tannenbaum

O Tan - nen - baum, o Tan - nen - baum, wie treu sind dei - ne
O Tan - nen - baum, o Tan - nen - baum, du kannst mir sehr ge -
O Tan - nen - baum, o Tan - nen - baum, dein Kleid will mich was

Blät - ter! Du grünst nicht nur zur Som - mers - zeit nein
fal - len. Wie oft hat nicht zur Weih - nachts - zeit ein
leh - ren. Die Hoff - nung und Be - stän - dig - keit gibt

auch im Win - ter, wenn es schneit. O Tan - nen - baum, o
Baum von dir mich hoch er - freut. O Tan - nen - baum, o
Trost und Kraft zu je - der Zeit. O Tan - nen - baum, o

Tan - nen - baum, wie treu sind dei - ne Blät - ter!
Tan - nen - baum, du kannst mir sehr ge - fal - len.
Tan - nen - baum, dein Kleid will mich was leh - ren.

A **Charts**

Chart 1. English Consonants

	Bilabial	Labiodental	Dental	Alveolar	Prepalatal	Palatal	Velar	Glottal
Stops								
voiced	[b]			[d]			[g]	
voiceless	[p]			[t]			[k]	
Fricatives								
voiced		[v]	[ð]	[z]	[ʒ]			
voiceless		[f]	[θ]	[s]	[ʃ]			[h]
Affricates								
voiced					[dʒ]			
voiceless					[tʃ]			
Nasals								
voiced	[m]			[n]			[ŋ]	
Laterals								
voiced				[l]				
Trills								
voiced				[ɾ]				
Retroflex								
voiced				[r]				
Glides								
voiced	[w]					[j]		

Chart 2. German Consonants

	Bilabial	Labiodental	Dental	Alveolar	Prepalatal	Palatal	Velar	Glottal
Stops								
voiced	[b]			[d]			[g]	
voiceless	[p]			[t]			[k]	[ǀ]
Fricatives								
voiced		[v]	[z]		[ʒ]			
voiceless		[f]	[s]		[ʃ]	[ç]	[χ]	[h]
Affricates								
voiced								
voiceless		[pf]		[ts]	[tʃ]			
Nasals								
voiced	[m]			[n]			[ŋ]	
Laterals								
voiced			[l]					
Trills								
voiced				[ɾ]				
Glides								
voiced						[j]		

Chart 3. English Vowels

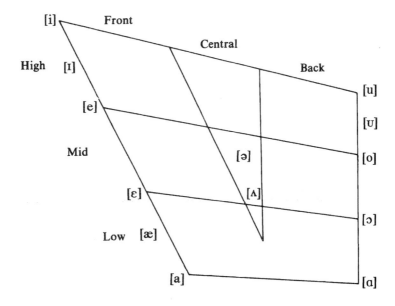

Chart 4. German Vowels

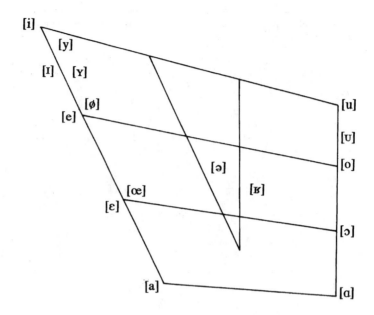

B Additional Song Texts

Brahms *Vergebliches Ständchen*

Guten Abend, mein Schatz,
Guten Abend, mein Kind!
Ich komm' aus Lieb' zu dir,
Ach, mach' mir auf die Tür!
Mach' mir auf die Tür!

"Mein' Tür ist verschlossen,
Ich lass' dich nicht ein;
Mutter die rät mir klug,
Wärst du herein mit Fug,
Wär's mit mir vorbei!"

So kalt ist die Nacht,
So eisig der Wind,
Daß mir das Herz erfriert,
Mein' Lieb' erlöschen wird;
Öffne mir, mein Kind!

"Löschet dein' Lieb'
Laß sie löschen nur!
Löschet sie immer zu,
Geh' heim zu Bett zur Ruh',
Gute Nacht, mein Knab'!"

FOLK SONG

Schubert *An die Musik*

Du holde Kunst, in wieviel grauen Stunden,
Wo mich des Lebens wilder Kreis umstrickt,
Hast du mein Herz zu warmer Lieb' entzunden,
Hast mich in eine bessre Welt entrückt!

Oft hat ein Seufzer, deiner Harf' entflossen,
Ein süßer, heiliger Akkord von dir,

Den Himmel bessrer Zeiten mir erschlossen,
Du holde Kunst, ich danke dir dafür!

SCHOBER

Du bist die Ruh'

Du bist die Ruh',
Der Friede mild,
Die Sehnsucht du,
Und was sie stillt.

Ich weihe dir
Voll Lust und Schmerz
Zur Wohnung hier
Mein Aug' und Herz.

Kehr ein bei mir
Und schließe du
Still hinter dir
Die Pforten zu!

Treib andern Schmerz
Aus dieser Brust!
Voll sei dies Herz
Von deiner Lust.

Dies Augenzelt
Von deinem Glanz
Allein erhellt,
O füll es ganz!

RÜCKERT

Erlkönig

Wer reitet so spät durch Nacht und Wind?
Es ist der Vater mit seinem Kind;
Er hat den Knaben wohl in dem Arm,
Er faßt ihn sicher, er hält ihn warm.

Mein Sohn, was birgst du so bang dein Gesicht?—
Siehst, Vater, du den Erlkönig nicht?
Den Erlenkönig mit Kron' und Schweif?—
Mein Sohn, es ist ein Nebelstreif.—

"Du liebes Kind, komm, geh mit mir!
Gar schöne Spiele spiel' ich mit dir,
Manch bunte Blumen sind an dem Strand,
Meine Mutter hat manch gülden Gewand."

Mein Vater, mein Vater, und hörest du nicht,
Was Erlenkönig mir leise verspricht?—
Sei ruhig, bleibe ruhig, mein Kind:
In dürren Blättern säuselt der Wind.—

"Willst, feiner Knabe, du mit mir gehn?
Meine Töchter sollen dich warten schön;
Meine Töchter führen den nächtlichen Reihn
Und wiegen und tanzen und singen dich ein."

Mein Vater, mein Vater, und siehst du nicht dort
Erlkönigs Töchter am düstern Ort?—
Mein Sohn, mein Sohn, ich seh' es genau:
Es scheinen die alten Weiden so grau.—

"Ich liebe dich, mich reizt deine schöne Gestalt;
Und bist du nicht willig, so brauch' ich Gewalt."
Mein Vater, mein Vater, jetzt faßt er mich an!
Erlkönig hat mir ein Leids getan!—

Dem Vater grauset's, er reitet geschwind,
Er hält in Armen das ächzende Kind,
Erreicht den Hof mit Mühe und Not;
In seinen Armen das Kind war tot.

GOETHE

Die Forelle

In einem Bächlein helle,
Da schoß in froher Eil'
Die launische Forelle
Vorüber wie ein Pfeil.
Ich stand an dem Gestade,
Und sah in süßer Ruh'
Des muntern Fischleins Bade
Im klaren Bächlein zu.

Ein Fischer mit der Rute
Wohl an dem Ufer stand,
Und sah's mit kaltem Blute,
Wie sich das Fischlein wand.
So lang dem Wasser helle,
So dacht' ich, nicht gebricht,
So fängt er die Forelle
Mit seiner Angel nicht.

Doch plötzlich ward dem Diebe
Die Zeit zu lang. Er macht
Das Bächlein tückisch trübe,

Und eh' ich es gedacht;—
So zuckte seine Rute,
Das Fischlein zappelt dran,
Und ich mit regem Blute
Sah die Betrogne an.

SCHUBART

Gretchen am Spinnrade

Meine Ruh ist hin,
Mein Herz ist schwer;
Ich finde sie nimmer
Und nimmermehr.

Wo ich ihn nicht hab'
Ist mir das Grab,
Die ganze Welt
Ist mir vergällt.

Mein armer Kopf
Ist mir verrückt,
Mein armer Sinn
Ist mir zerstückt.

Meine Ruh ist hin,
Mein Herz ist schwer;
Ich finde sie nimmer
Und nimmermehr.

Nach ihm nur schau' ich
Zum Fenster hinaus,
Nach ihm nur geh'ich
Aus dem Haus.

Sein hoher Gang,
Sein' edle Gestalt,
Seines Mundes Lächeln,
Seiner Augen Gewalt,

Und seiner Rede
Zauberfluß,
Sein Händedruck,
Und ach, sein Kuß!

Meine Ruh ist hin,
Mein Herz ist schwer;
Ich finde sie nimmer
Und nimmermehr.

Mein Busen drängt
Sich nach ihm hin;
Ach, dürft' ich fassen
Und halten ihn

Und küssen ihn,
So wie ich wollt',
An seinen Küssen
Vergehen sollt'!

GOETHE

Die junge Nonne

Wie braust durch die Wipfel der heulende Sturm!
Es klirren die Balken, es zittert das Haus!
Es rollet der Donner, es leuchtet der Blitz,
Und finster die Nacht wie das Grab!

Immerhin, immerhin,
So tobt' es auch jüngst noch in mir!
Es brauste das Leben, wie jetzo der Sturm,
Es bebten die Glieder, wie jetzo das Haus,
Es flammte die Liebe, wie jetzo der Blitz,
Und finster die Brust wie das Grab!

Nun tobe, du wilder, gewalt'ger Sturm,
Im Herzen ist Friede, im Herzen ist Ruh',
Des Bräutigams harret die liebende Braut,
Gereinigt in prüfender Glut,
Der ewigen Liebe getraut.

Ich harre, mein Heiland, mit sehnendem Blick!
Komm, himmlischer Bräutigam, hole die Braut,
Erlöse die Seele von irdischer Haft!
Horch, friedlich ertönet das Glöcklein vom Turm!
Es lockt mich das süße Getön
Allmächtig zu ewigen Höh'n.
Alleluja!

CRAIGHER

Der Tod und das Mädchen

DAS MÄDCHEN

Vorüber, ach vorüber
Geh, wilder Knochenmann!
Ich bin noch jung! Geh, Lieber,
Und rühre mich nicht an!

DER TOD

Gib deine Hand, du schön und zart Gebild!
Bin Freund und komme nicht zu strafen.
Sei gutes Muts! Ich bin nicht wild!
Sollst sanft in meinen Armen schlafen!

CLAUDIUS

Wohin?

Ich hört' ein Bächlein rauschen
Wohl aus dem Felsenquell,
Hinab zum Tale rauschen
So frisch und wunderhell.

Ich weiß nicht, wie mir wurde,
Nicht, wer den Rat mir gab,
Ich mußte gleich hinunter
Mit meinem Wanderstab.

Hinunter und immer weiter,
Und immer dem Bache nach,
Und immer frischer rauschte,
Und immer heller der Bach.

Ist das denn meine Straße?
O Bächlein, sprich, wohin?
Du hast mit deinem Rauschen
Mir ganz berauscht den Sinn.

Was sag' ich denn vom Rauschen?
Das kann kein Rauschen sein!
Es singen wohl die Nixen
Tief unten ihren Reihn.

Laß singen, Gesell, laß rauschen,
Und wandre fröhlich nach!
Es gehn ja Mühlenräder
In jedem klaren Bach.

MÜLLER

Schumann *Du bist wie eine Blume*

Du bist wie eine Blume
So hold und schön und rein;
Ich schau' dich an, und Wehmut
Schleicht mir ins Herz hinein.

Mir ist, als ob ich die Hände
Aufs Haupt dir legen sollt'

Betend, daß Gott dich erhalte
So rein und schön und hold.

HEINE

Du Ring an meinem Finger

Du Ring an meinem Finger,
Mein goldenes Ringelein,
Ich drücke dich fromm an die Lippen,
Dich fromm an das Herze mein.

Ich hatt' ihn ausgeträumet,
Der Kindheit friedlichen Traum,
Ich fand allein mich verloren
Im öden, unendlichen Raum.

Du Ring an meinem Finger,
Da hast du mich erst belehrt,
Hast meinem Blick erschlossen
Des Lebens unendlichen Wert.

Ich werd' ihm dienen, ihm leben,
Ihm angehören ganz,
Hin selber mich geben und finden
Verklärt mich in seinem Glanz.

Du Ring an meinem Finger,
Mein goldenes Ringelein,
Ich drücke dich fromm an die Lippen,
Dich fromm an das Herze mein.

CHAMISSO

Frühlingsnacht

Überm Garten durch die Lüfte
Hör' ich Wandervögel ziehn,
Das bedeutet Frühlingsdüfte,
Unten fängt's schon an zu blühn.

Jauchzen möcht' ich, möchte weinen,
Ist mir's doch, als könnt's nicht sein,
Alte Wunder wieder scheinen
Mit dem Mondesglanz herein.

Und der Mond, die Sterne sagen's,
Und im Traume rauscht's der Hain,
Und die Nachtigallen schlagen's:
Sie ist deine, sie ist dein!

EICHENDORFF

Ich grolle nicht

Ich grolle nicht, und wenn das Herz auch bricht,
Ewig verlor'nes Lieb! ich grolle nicht.
Wie du auch strahlst in Diamantenpracht,
Es fällt kein Strahl in deines Herzens Nacht.

Das weiß ich längst. Ich sah dich ja im Traume,
Und sah die Nacht in deines Herzens Raume,
Und sah die Schlang', die dir am Herzen frißt,
Ich sah, mein Lieb, wie sehr du elend bist.
Ich grolle nicht.

HEINE

Die Lotosblume

Die Lotosblume ängstigt
Sich vor der Sonne Pracht,
Und mit gesenktem Haupte
Erwartet sie träumend die Nacht.

Der Mond, der ist ihr Buhle,
Er weckt sie mit seinem Licht,
Und ihm entschleiert sie freundlich
Ihr frommes Blumengesicht.

Sie blüht und glüht und leuchtet
Und starret stumm in die Höh';
Sie duftet und weinet und zittert
Vor Liebe und Liebesweh.

HEINE

Mondnacht

Es war, als hätt' der Himmel
Die Erde still geküßt,
Daß sie im Blütenschimmer,
Von ihm nur träumen müßt'.

Die Luft ging durch die Felder,
Die Ähren wogten sacht,
Es rauschten leis die Wälder,
So sternklar war die Nacht.

Und meine Seele spannte
Weit ihre Flügel aus,
Flog durch die stillen Lande,
Als flöge sie nach Haus.

EICHENDORFF

Strauss *Traum durch die Dämmerung*

Weite Wiesen im Dämmergrau;
Die Sonne verglomm, die Sterne ziehn;
Nun geh' ich zu der schönsten Frau,
Weit über Wiesen im Dämmergrau,
Tief in den Busch von Jasmin.

Durch Dämmergrau in der Liebe Land;
Ich gehe nicht schnell, ich eile nicht;
Mich zieht ein weiches, samtenes Band
Durch Dämmergrau in der Liebe Land,
In ein blaues, mildes Licht.

BIERBAUM

Morgen

Und Morgen wird die Sonne wieder scheinen,
Und auf dem Wege, den ich gehen werde,
Wird uns, die Seligen, sie wieder einen,
Inmitten dieser sonnenatmenden Erde . . .

Und zu dem Strand, dem weiten, wogenblauen,
Werden wir still und langsam niedersteigen.
Stumm werden wir uns in die Augen schauen,
Und auf uns sinkt des Glückes stummes Schweigen.

MACKAY

Wolf *Anakreons Grab*

Wo die Rose hier blüht, wo Reben um Lorbeer sich schlingen,
Wo das Turtelchen lockt, wo sich das Grillchen ergötzt,
Welch ein Grab ist hier, das alle Götter mit Leben
Schön bepflanzt und geziert? Es ist Anakreons Ruh'.
Frühling, Sommer und Herbst genoß der glückliche Dichter;
Vor dem Winter hat ihn endlich der Hügel geschützt.

GOETHE

Er ist's

Frühling läßt sein blaues Band
Wieder flattern durch die Lüfte;
Süße, wohlbekannte Düfte
Streifen ahnungsvoll das Land.
Veilchen träumen schon,
Wollen balde kommen.

—Horch, von fern ein leiser Harfenton!
Frühling, ja du bist's!
Dich hab' ich vernommen!

MÖRIKE

Mignon—1

Kennst du das Land, wo die Zitronen blühn,
Im dunkein Laub die Gold-Orangen glühn,
Ein sanfter Wind vom blauen Himmel weht,
Die Myrte still und hoch der Lorbeer steht?
Kennst du es wohl?—Dahin! Dahin!
Möcht' ich mit dir, o mein Geliebter, ziehn.

Kennst du das Haus? Auf Säulen ruht sein Dach,
Es glänzt der Saal, es schimmert das Gemach,
Und Marmorbilder stehn und sehn mich an:

Was hat man dir, du armes Kind, getan?
Kennst du es wohl?—Dahin! Dahin!
Möcht' ich mit dir, o mein Beschützer, ziehn.

Kennst du den Berg und seinen Wolkensteg?
Das Maultier sucht im Nebel seinen Weg;
In Höhlen wohnt der Drachen alte Brut;
Es stürzt der Fels und über ihn die Flut.
Kennst du ihn wohl?—Dahin! Dahin
Geht unser Weg; o Vater, laß uns ziehn!

GOETHE

Mignon—3

Nur wer die Sehnsucht kennt,
Weiß, was ich leide!
Allein und abgetrennt
Von aller Freude
Seh' ich ans Firmament
Nach jener Seite.
Ach! der mich liebt und kennt,
Ist in der Weite.
Es schwindelt mir, es brennt
Mein Eingeweide.
Nur wer die Sehnsucht kennt
Weiß was ich leide!

GOETHE

Verborgenheit

Laß, o Welt, o laß mich sein!
Locket nicht mit Liebesgaben,
Laßt dies Herz alleine haben
Seine Wonne, seine Pein!

Was ich traure, weiß ich nicht,
Es ist unbekanntes Wehe;
Immerdar durch Tränen sehe
Ich der Sonne liebes Licht.

Oft bin ich mir kaum bewußt,
Und die helle Freude zücket
Durch die Schwere, die mich drücket,
Wonniglich in meiner Brust.

Laß, o Welt, o laß mich sein!
Locket nicht mit Liebesgaben,
Laßt dies Herz alleine haben
Seine Wonne, seine Pein!

MÖRIKE

Das verlassene Mägdlein

Früh, wann die Hähne krähn,
Eh' die Sternlein schwinden,
Muß ich am Herde stehn,
Muß Feuer zünden.

Schön ist der Flammen Schein,
Es springen die Funken;
Ich schaue so drein,
In Leid versunken.

Plötzlich, da kommt es mir,
Treuloser Knabe,
Daß ich die Nacht von dir
Geträumet habe.

Träne auf Träne dann
Stürzet hernieder;
So kommt der Tag heran—
O ging' er wieder!

MÖRIKE

C German Pronunciation of Latin

In traditional German diction, the rules for pronunciation of Latin are essentially the same as those for the pronunciation of German.

VOWELS

A. *e, i, o, u,* and *y*

In stressed syllables, the vowels *e, i, o, u,* and *y* are, as in German, pronounced closed before a single consonant and open before two or more consonants.

1. *e*
   a. stressed *e*
      1) closed [e]: *confitemur* [kɔnfi'temur]
      2) open [ɛ]: *terra* ['tɛɾa]
         exceptions: *et* [ɛt]
                     per [pɛɾ]
                     es [ɛs]
   b. unstressed *e*
   As in German, unstressed *e* is almost always pronounced [ə]: *sedes* ['zedəs], *extolle* [ɛks'tɔlə]

2. *i*
   a. closed [i]: *filium* ['filium]
   b. open [ɪ]: *Christus* ['kɾɪstus]

3. *o*
   a. closed [o]: *gloria* ['gloɾia]
   b. open [ɔ]: *orbem* ['ɔrbəm]

4. *u*
   a. closed [u]: *tuam* ['tuɑm]
   b. open [ʊ]: *mundi* ['mʊndi]

5. *y* (recall that in German *y* is pronounced like *ü*)
closed [y]: *kyrie* ['kyɾiɛ]

B. *a, ae, oe*

1. *a*
a is always pronounced [a]: *peccata* [pɛ'kata]

2. *ae*
The vowel *ae* is always pronounced [ɛ] (recall that German *ä*—which is always pronounced [ɛ]—is sometimes spelled *ae*): *aeternum* [ɛ'tɛɾnum], *gloriae* ['gloɾiɛ]

3. *oe*
The vowel *oe* is always pronounced [ø] (recall that German *ö*—pronounced [ø]— is sometimes spelled *oe*): *coeli* ['tsøli].

CONSONANTS

1. *c*
As in German, *c* is pronounced [ts] before a front vowel: *coeli* ['tsøli] and [k] before a back vowel: *magnificat* [mag'nifikat].

2. *g*
g is always pronounced [g]: *Virgines* ['vɪɾginis], *regna* ['ɾegna]

3. *h*
In initial position, *h* is always pronounced: *hominem* ['hominəm]

4. *s*
As in German, *s* is always voiced before a vowel; otherwise it is voiceless: *sanctus* ['zaŋktus].

5. *x*
As in German, *x* is pronounced [ks]: *exercitus* [ɛksɛɾ'tsitus].

6. *qu*
As in German, *qu* is pronounced [kv]: *quoque* ['kvokvə].

7. *t*
t is always pronounced [t]—even (unlike German) in the combination *ti*: *deprecationem* [dɛpɾɛkati'onəm]